Follow

Your

Dreams!

Then

Now

Preface

  In 1983, at the age of sixteen, I entered the wonderful beauty industry, and immediately, I had a vision of owning a salon one day. I knew that owning a salon could not happen overnight, and I needed to have some experience before this dream could be fulfilled. Over the years, I was able to advance to different levels within the business. Many years of persistence led me from shampoo girl to assistant, assistant to stylist, and then from stylist to owner/educator. I want my passion for this business to motivate future hairstylists, or those already in the field, to explore many avenues within the fields of beauty and fashion. I will offer you ways to succeed as a hairstylist, cosmetologist, or salon owner, and I will provide suggestions, tips, and guidelines that I have learned along the way. This book will give you an insight to experiences that are unique to working in a hair salon environment. It has always been my desire to change lives through hairstyles and cosmetology, one client at a time. I sincerely hope that what you read in the chapters ahead will inspire and encourage you to pursue your dreams surrounding your career choices and your daily life. This book was designed to not only give you the knowhow for the salon industry, but also to share ideas of balancing life, work, relationships, and family. So if you are a man or a woman who is interested in: personal growth, improving the quality of service in the workplace, learning how to increase sales, retaining clients, and staying energized by your work, then I suggest you get yourself a copy of this book and embrace a new chapter in your life.

Passion

Table of Contents

WOMEN'S SMALL BUSINESS ASSOCIATION, LLC.

AWARD

2012 Best Business Woman
of the Year Award

Foreword

Jacqueline Capatolla has become the inspiration for so many women in Pittsburgh, as she continues to demonstrate the drive and resilience needed to be an entrepreneur in today's economy. Her constant support of women in the "startup" process of starting their business has earned her the respect of so many.

Susan Miller, WSBA Founder and President
Women's Small Business Association, LLC
www.WSBA.ws

<u>**Recommendations for Jacqueline Capatolla**</u>

It is an absolute honor to have met and established a business relationship with Jacqueline. Jacqueline is a distributor for our Cosmetic products. She is a successful owner of two salons and is repeatedly one of the top salon distributors in our company. With her vast product knowledge as well as industry expertise, she has proven to be a leader in the beauty and cosmetology arena. She is a successful female entrepreneur and mentor to women in the Pittsburgh area. I would give Jacqueline's book the highest recommendation to anyone interested in pursuing a career in the beauty and fashion industry.

- Tiffany Fluhme,
Fluhme Cosmetics
http://www.fluhme.com

✕ ✕

Jacqueline's House of Beauty has been an active member of the Brookline Chamber of Commerce since 1994, she took on the task of chairing a Wedding Planner guide in 2010. Great to have such a successful business in the Brookline Community.

- Linda Boss,
President, Brookline Chamber of Commerce
938 Brookline Boulevard, Pittsburgh, PA 15226

✕ ✕

Jackie Capatolla is an inspiration. She is without a doubt one of the kindest, most sincere people I have ever met. She also happens to be an expert in her field, always on top of what's new in the industry and eager to share her knowledge with staff and clients. She has so much to give and I am thrilled that she has finally written a book! Can't wait for the next one!

- Gina Hussar, Editor-in-Chief
FrontRow Monthly
http://frontrowmonthly.com

✕ ✕

Working with Jacqueline is never work...her perseverance, drive, diligence and passion in all that she does inspires those around her. This [woman] gives a gentle push [and] also motivates those around her. Through her salon, the Inside Out initiative and fashion affiliated events she has given her time. Pittsburgh fashion week can call on JACQUELINE'S salon and they're right there to deliver. Our mission is parallel to raise awareness of fashion by giving back to it.

- Miyoshi Anderson
Executive Director and founder of Pittsburgh Fashion Week.
www.pittsburghfashionweek.com

✕ ✕

I have worked side by side with Jacqueline for almost nine years. During that time we have laughed and cried together. This book is filled with her experiences, her inspiration, and her heart and soul. I recommend it for anyone involved in the beauty and fashion industry or anyone else who needs encouragement and motivation to excel in their life and business.

- JoAnne Bolla
Salon Manager

Using the services at JACQUELINE'S salon in the Grant building is a convenient way to get your hair and makeup done while taking a stress break from work. Jackie Capatolla did a wonderful job. The Fluhme makeup she used blends well and is safe for my sensitive skin. The eye shadow palette contained bold colors that can be brushed on lightly or heavily making the transition from day to night. I felt confident with my new appearance and received quite a few compliments due to the job great job Jackie did. Thank you Jackie!

Jillian M.

Clients Who Love Their Hair

Create a "look book" portfolio.

Introduction

Hello and welcome! My name is Jacqueline Capatolla. I have been in the beauty and fashion industry since 1983 when, at the age of sixteen, I was volunteering as a shampoo girl for a high-end downtown salon in Pittsburgh, Pennsylvania. I learned the ropes and my way around the salon, and I found my entry-level position to be so exciting and energizing, and it was a great introduction to my future career.

Twenty-seven years after working at my first job in a hair salon, I opened my own shop in the downtown area of Pittsburgh, PA, so I feel I have come full circle. I also continue to own and operate my first salon, which is located in a community that is south of the downtown area.

This career journey has been truly exceptional, and I feel that I have been extremely blessed to be working in a profession that I find to be exciting nearly three decades beyond my first job as a hair stylist. I also feel very honored to be an entrepreneur who has the ability to create opportunities for others.

I have always written down my thoughts and ideas over the years, and after reviewing all of my notes, I had the urge to write this book. I wanted to be able to share with you my experiences and knowledge that I have gained through this process over the past 29 years. The purpose of this book is to truly inspire you to follow your dreams and your passion. The past three years of writing this book have been very rewarding to me personally. I have been able to see all that I have accomplished during my career through hard work and perseverance. This book is really for anyone who is interested in starting a business or anyone who wants to be successful in their career path. The beauty industry is close to my heart, so I chose to write about this particular business. However, this book can be an inspiration for someone who has thoughts about starting any type of business and for anyone who has the drive and ambition to be self-employed someday.

My inspiration comes from all the beauty in the world and my experiences and knowledge of hairstyling and cosmetology is what led me to share my dreams with you. After three years of preparing notes for this book, I feel very grateful to be able to finally share my experiences with others. Writing this book has brought me a sense of joy, fulfillment, and peace. It is my hope that you will find the same satisfaction in your career and in the rewards of a job well done. I feel very blessed to be living the American dream, and I remain optimistic that it is still possible.

Follow Your Passions and Dreams

We all have a passion and desire to pursue some goal in life. When I was little I used to love to pretend that I had a beauty salon and I would style my dolls' hair. I would braid, shampoo, dry and clip the hair on my dolls, and this gave me a sense of accomplishment. As time went on, I took an interest in fixing my own hair. Sharing the bathroom mirror with three other sisters was always a challenge. They were always yelling at me to hurry up. All four girls shared a bedroom, so as you can imagine, space was limited. As I entered high school, the thought of one day working in a salon and someday owning a salon business stayed with me. My friends and family would want me to style their hair if they were attending a special event. As I previously mentioned, I volunteered as a shampoo girl in a prestigious downtown Pittsburgh salon. What a great experience it was for me! I learned the foundations for my career and the basics of the industry. There was never a doubt in my mind that I wanted to pursue this profession. I entered Pittsburgh Beauty Academy right after high school. My boyfriend (who later became my husband) went away to college, and I knew that it was my time to focus on my passion and future. We all have a dream. What is yours?

Once you realize which career you would like to pursue, you must ask yourself if you have the passion and the desire to one day have your own business. If so, firmly believe that you can make that happen. Opportunities can unfold in the right time in your life. Try to be patient and learn all you can about the field or career path you have chosen, no matter what that may be. You may want to be a florist, a restaurant owner, a designer, or a fitness instructor. Dare to dream of owning your own shop, restaurant, or studio at some point. Timing is everything. Once you have acquired the knowledge, skills, and experience, you will know when you are ready to proceed to the next level of owning a business. You may need to patiently wait until you are more financially prepared to start a business, or maybe you need to get other personal goals in order, but it is important that you take your time and feel good about your decision. We all walk on stepping stones to reach our goals in life, and eventually we find what it is that we are destined to do.

As you read through the chapters, take note of the promotional ideas that I have used, think outside the box, and see how you can compare your own ideas with mine. Focus on what type of business you may be interested in and passionate about. Keep an open mind about how one business can lead you into another. Use my steps that I have taken and be inspired to take your own steps to a brighter future.

I want the contents of this book to give you the incentive to challenge the inner you. Find out who you are as a salon professional or any type of business owner. Take time to really listen to your thoughts and emotions, evaluate them and be aware of how they make you feel. I hope that this journey inspires you to be a better person inside and out and to pass that along to your clients. Thank you for taking the time to explore the process of: continuing your education as a cosmetologist, searching for your first job, and polishing your skills to work as a stylist with the possibility of one day owing a hair salon.

God bless ~ Jacqueline

Enjoy!!

Journey

Acknowledgments

To my husband, Pat, and my son, Patric for all of your hard work with maintaining the salon and for all of your love and support!

To my daughter Shaylee, who helped take my salons to the next level as the marketing director of the salon. I'm so grateful to have the opportunity to work with my daughter, and I thank you for your love and support!

To my sister Lynn, without you none of this would have been possible. Thank you! Thank you! Thank you!

To my Salon Manager, JoAnne Bolla, for your great organizational skills in the daily management of the salon. My business is successful because of your dedication. You're the best!

To Victor Solomon, along with JoAnne Bolla, you are both vital parts of my team, and I thank you for your continuing support and dedication. Your skills, talents, and hard work are an inspiration to me!

To all my staff, past, present, and future, you've helped me to grow and succeed. Thank you for being part of Jacqueline's Salon!

To Fedora, who is always there to cheer me on and give me encouragement. She believes in me and makes me laugh and always supports me.

To Jordan, who helped me so much with this journey and never complained, even with all my crazy notes! To Bethany for directing my thoughts about writing a book

To Maggie Cauley for manuscript editing and preparation. Thank you, Maggie, for all your hard work, I could not have done this without you. All of the time and effort you put into the editing is beyond words. Thank you for all your support and belief in me and this book!

Katrina, I love the beautiful cover that you designed! Thank you!

To all the cosmetologists out there who have a dream and passion for this industry, I wish you all the best!

To Tiffany, Susan, Linda, and Gina, Miyoshi, and JoAnne for your kind words and your encouragement!

Dedication

To all 32 of my family members, my parents, my brother and sisters, my husband and my children, and to all of my in-laws. Thank you for your love and support!

This book is dedicated to all of my family members.

My family members are the clients that never complain, but they are also the clients who are always looking for that last minute appointment. I guess this goes a long with the job. I come from a very big family, and a loud one at that! Italians are just that way and that's how we show our love. The Irish side of my personality is a little calmer. You always know when my oldest sister walks into the salon; you can just hear her all the way in the back. My family is my rock, without them I would not be the person I am today. I have been blessed. My father always told me to keep plugging away and that is what I do. My mother has always said to get up and get moving and now I tell the same thing to my kids. Mom and Dad, thank you for taking the time to teach me the important lessons in life and for your unconditional love. My sisters are always there when I need them and my brother is there as well. Even though my brother is the only boy surrounded by four sisters, he truly was not spoiled. One of my fondest memories of our early lives happened on a day when I was a freshman in high school and he was a senior. I fainted in the lunch room during the first week of school, and I woke up to find him kicking me and telling me to get up! I guess his little sister embarrassed him. In all seriousness, he always looked out for me and still does! My husband listens to all of my ideas, and he always encourages me. He truly is my wing and gives me strength, love, and support each and every day. I love you!

My children often get tired of hearing me lecture to them, but I know they are listening. They are absolutely my inspiration and such a beautiful gift from God. You both are my world! I have great support from of all my extended family members. I want to thank my nieces, nephews, and all of my in-laws for all of your love and reassurance. I have a lot of people in my life, and you are all my joy and comfort. So, I guess my family members really pay for haircuts with love. All of us need the love and support of family, friends, teachers, or mentors to succeed in life. I want to thank you all of you for being there for me!

The love and support of
family, friends, and mentors
will help you to succeed!

In loving memory of my brother-in-law, George

What an inspiration you were to me. The love you gave to your family and friends was incredible! George, I thank you, most of all, for the love you gave to all of us You always took great care of our sister and nephews, and my parents adored you for being the best son-in-law, the best father to your children, and the best uncle to my children. We will never forget your love and we all miss you more than words can say! Your sense of humor and your ability to make us all feel safe and welcomed will never be forgotten. We may no longer have you physically here with us, but you will always be present as a big bright light in our hearts! We will love you and miss you until we see you again.

Thank you for always inspiring me to be a better person and for giving me encouragement and support in all of my adventures. Having a brother-in-law like you was a blessing from God, and I'm so thankful that you were a part of my life. This book is in memory of you, George,

Love,

Jackie

Chapter 1

Ten Steps to Getting Started

1. Believe in Yourself
2. Having a Dream
3. Continuing Education
4. Building a Team
5. Developing Relationships
6. Create a Plan of Action - State Board, Laws, Applications
7. Having a Vision and a Mission
8. Business Plan Overview
9. Calendar of Events - New Beginnings – Each Season Inspires New Styles
10. Always Stay True to Yourself and Let Your Vision and Mission Lead the Way

Step 1. Believe in yourself.

We all have times when we want to try new things in life, and a little voice in the back of our minds says, *No, you can't do that.* You know you need to press on and ignore that little voice and believe in yourself. We need to have faith and take a chance as long as it is a reasonable one. Believing in yourself can be very hard work. Once you choose a goal, you need to make sure it is really what you want, and do not rush in to it. Make careful choices. Weigh the pros and cons about any decisions that make you hesitate to move forward. You may believe in attempting to try something new, but are you ready to make it happen? Have confidence in your abilities, and good things will begin to come your way.

Step 2. Having a dream.

It all starts when you are little and you see something that catches your attention, something that makes you go, *Wow!* Think back to that excited feeling that made you feel so good about yourself. Apply that excitement to your career aspirations, and you can make them a reality. You will love your life. It makes you feel as if God put you here to do great things and you now know and understand what they are. Never give up, have the desire, be positive. Have a dream and make it happen.

Let's get started!

Step 3. Continuing Education.

Even the best student in the classroom still has to learn, read, and take time to do some research. You are never too educated, too old, or too over-extended to learn. Keeping up with the changing trends and techniques will only add to your creative gifts and enable you to style the hair of your future clients. Our energetic society craves bold and eye-catching fads and trends. We live in a time of fast-paced changes. If we are excited about the fashion and beauty in our culture, we can convert that excitement into creative work and embrace new challenges. Times change, people change, but you are always you! Strive to be edgy, creative, and passionate. Be willing to grow and never stop learning!

A solid education will make you more confident in your work, and you will be knowledgeable when giving style and hair-care advice to your clients. Continuing your education will give you the power to grow, and it will also give you the means to grow. Creative people are always coming up with new ideas. Don't be left behind. Knowledge is the key to building a strong foundation, and begin course of study by learning the basics. As time goes on, you will feel more comfortable. Encourage yourself to keep finding ways to learn not only about your chosen profession but also about interests that are unrelated to your career.

Step 4. Building a Team.

Building a strong team of stylists, assistants, managers, marketing representatives, financial advisers, and front desk receptionists is the key to the success of any salon. While you are at work, your less visible team will also include family, friends, neighbors, and mentors. When you have good people around you in life, all things are possible. Keep the positive in and the negative out. If you have an assembly of good people with you, you will accomplish so much more. You should always work with people who believe in you and see the true beauty of what are creating. These are the ones you want to have near you because they have the same passion and drive that you have. Each member of your team will bring their individual talents and skills to the workplace. Your team members may all be doing different jobs, but their combined efforts form a solid foundation for your business. As a team, you will begin to realize that you are so much stronger as a group than alone. Structure, passion, and good people add up to the sum total of success.

Example:

At one time I had a really great assistant. This employee knew exactly what she needed to do to assist the stylists while they were working with their customers. She maintained our stations, laundered the towels, and did the necessary sweeping and cleaning in the salon. She knew that she didn't have the skills to be a stylist, and that assisting the stylists was her strong point. The shampoo girl, nail technician, assistant, stylist, educator, designer, manager, and salon owner, should work together to form a solid team within the salon. Everyone fits in somewhere. Once you have established your role on the team, perfect it, and take pride in your work.

Step 5. Developing Relationships.

Forming good relationships with your staff and clients will help you to succeed. You need to be able to relate to your coworkers, your clients, family, and friends. Maintaining healthy relationships will help you to grow as a person, as an individual, and as a stylist. If you are the lead stylist, you should share your knowledge with your coworkers. You should also remember that you can learn as much from them as they will learn from you. Be sure to respect and appreciate the people around you. We cannot do everything alone, and a network of good relationships will lead you to a fulfilling life.

Step 6. Create a Plan of Action.

Get all the state board forms, applications, and licenses in order. Whether you wish to be a stylist, be part of the team in management, or own a salon, it is up to you. Take on what you can handle. We all have different qualities that best fit us and our needs. Once you find your place in the industry, then you can develop a plan to attract and retain clients. Ask yourself how far you want to take your career. How much time, effort, and dedication are you willing to give to reach your goals? Creating a plan will keep you focused on all of the steps that you need to take as you launch your career. As you are getting things in order, decide if you should lead or follow, and set your goals.

Step 7. Having a vision and a mission.

We all have a picture in our mind of how we want things to go. When you have a vision, you need to see clearly. Look at the big picture and prepare to step into the future. Decide which path you will take, and plan how you will get there. Ask yourself the following questions:

- What are you trying to accomplish?
- How do you want your plan to take shape?
- What are the most important goals you are trying to achieve?

The mission is for you to figure out why you are doing what you are doing. If you have a vision and mission, they will give you hope and something to aim for. In time, any thoughts and ideas of your future that may have been confusing, or caused doubt, will become clear and you will know which direction to take.

Step 8. Business Plan - Overview

Lots of decisions will need to be made before you put a business plan together.

- The first is deciding how you want to establish your business.
- You will need to have a location. How many square feet will you need?
- What services will you be offering?
- What type of salon are you going for? Modern? Contemporary?
- Decide on products, equipment, distributors, employees, finances, taxes, and accounting.

This process can be overwhelming, and it is normal for you to feel as though your head is spinning. Keep pushing through things, and one day it all comes together, and before you know it you are off to a great start. You should begin planning your business by making a handwritten outline of how you envision your salon will look. Your outline should contain your thoughts about the location and size of your future business, the products and styling tools you will need to purchase, your ideas about décor, and the salon image that you want to project to your customers.

So, I know that you are wondering how much does it cost to get your business up and running? Well, the answer to this question depends upon how much are you able to spend. You can be set and ready to go with a practical two-chair salon, or you can choose to go all out and have a twenty-chair salon featuring lots of bling, bells, and whistles. The possibilities are endless, depending upon your vision and available resources for your salon. Before you open any type of business, it is necessary to review your finances to determine what you are able to afford. This is one part of your plan that deserves a great deal of attention. You will have many start-up costs when you open your salon. A small-business loan is an option to consider, and you should check into government loans for small businesses as well.

When you are preparing to open your salon, you will need to make sure all your cosmetology legal documents are in place. You will be inspected prior to opening your business. Both of my salons meet Pennsylvania state requirements. Each state has different regulations, but most will be the same.

You will need a long checklist of supplies to review as you are preparing to open your doors. Some items that you will need to purchase are a first aid kit, a fire extinguisher, and jars of disinfectant solutions for each station. You will need a cosmetology license and a license for your place of business. Your salon will also need to have a proper commercial zoning permit. No matter where you open a salon you must register with the state and follow the regulations. This process can take some time to complete, so make sure you start early when proceeding with a plan of action.

You can check your state for different qualifications. Some states offer booth rental and some do not. Make sure that you go through the checklist and have everything in order before you have your inspection. You will be fined by the state if you do not comply with mandatory State Board of Cosmetology laws.

You will need to register the name of your business with the Internal Revenue Service for tax purposes. You can register online, and once you have completed the form, you will be assigned an Employee Identification Number (E.I.N.). This number is also referred to as a Federal Identification Number.

When you are planning to open your salon, you will need to assess what types of customers will make up your client base and how you will be marketing to a group of clients who may vary in age and sense of style.

Step 9. Calendar of Events - New Beginnings – Each Season Inspires New Styles

Having an event planner will keep you on track. Use some or all of my promotional ideas. Combine product and service promotions together, and have contests. Event calendars add excitement to each season for the staff and for the clients. Make your promotions fun and attractive in order to keep clients interested.

Seasonal Marketing and Promoting Examples:

March	October 1, 2012
St. Patrick's Day	Fall Festival / Halloween

Step 10. Staying True to Yourself.

As you enter the beauty industry, or any other business that you choose, you should begin to feel confident that you have everything in place. You have worked very hard up to this point, savor the moment! What a great feeling that is! Enjoy it, you have earned that. Make sure you give yourself reality checks. Be careful not to become distracted by anything that will come between you and your goals. Stay true to your vision and your mission. Remember, you were born with the talent and creativity that will help you to become a successful entrepreneur. You can make this happen. All you need is to do is believe in yourself. Enjoy the planning process and the rewards that will come to you in the future. You deserve it!

Celebration!

The beautiful roses came from my family in honor of my 10-year anniversary.

Chapter 2
Beauty School

Before choosing a beauty school, you should consider whether this career choice will be a good fit for you. You want to be able to take full advantage of this opportunity to continue your education so that you will sharpen your skills as a stylist. Do some researches of the academies in your area before you enroll in any school, and make sure the school is reputable. It would be wise to choose a school that is close to home or close to public transportation. When you schedule a visit to any school, take a complete tour and meet some of the instructors. Ask about the equipment that is used during training sessions. You should also ask to see their curriculum and make comparisons of what you find with other schools. Most schools follow a similar curricular schedule. The topics that will be covered are:

- Hair cleansing

- Cutting and styling

- Color and texture

- Basic skin care and esthetics

- Business development skills

- Retail training

- Makeup

- Anatomy

- Nails

- Chemistry and scalp analysis

- Customer relationship skills

Career Path

In general, a cosmetology license requires a nine-month course of study. A general cosmetologist will need 1,250-1,500 credit hours, and a nail technologist will need 200 credit hours. If you want to work toward a manager or teacher's license, the course will be extended to twelve months. It is important that you ask questions during your visit. Find out what the policy of the school would be about job placement, and ask if there is any assistance with resumes and portfolios. Tuition prices will vary, so find a school that will give you the most for your money. Ask what supplies and textbooks are covered by your tuition. If necessary, ask about financial aid programs, scholarships, or low-cost federal or private loans, or grants. An overview of the course would include: basic shampoo and consultation, hair anatomy, and hair chemistry.

Requirements:

- A high school diploma or GED – depends on the state where the school is located
- A minimum of nine months and 1,500 credits
- 250 hours before students can work on clinical services
- 200 theory and mannequin training hours
- 15 hours of skin care
- 10 hours of nail care
- 25 hours – on live models
- Class curriculum
- Theory
- Chemistry
- Sanitation / sterilization
- Permanent waving - chemistry
- Relaxers – chemistry
- Hair color chemistry
- Scalp treatment
- Shampooing
- Safety precautions – bleach products – electrical – tints – dyes
- Salesmanship
- Telephone etiquette and ethics

- Professional neatness

- Attitudes and friendliness

- Social skills / desk work – reception

- Hair removal

- Tweezing

- Waxing

- State Board of Cosmetology laws, rules, and regulations

 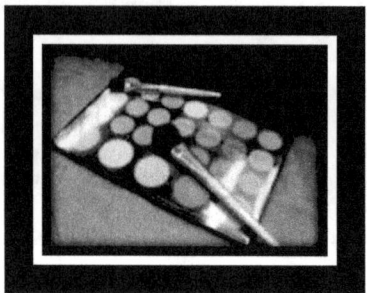 

After Graduation:

- State board examinations
    - Needed to get licensed
    - Perform on mannequin
    - Practice theory

> **Your toolbox is where it all begins. Your beauty school kit contains everything that you need for creative styling.**

Practice and Study:

- Visit State Board of Cosmetology website for all regulations and requirements

- http://www.portal.state.pa.us/portal/server.pt/community/state_board_of_cosmetology/12507

Your cosmetology kit will include the following items:

- Clips

- Combs

- Brushes

- Rollers

- Mannequin
- Shears
- Clippers
- Irons
- Perm rods
- Capes
- Mixing bowls
- Razors
- Blow dryer

Suggested Reading:

Fashion Magazines:

Behind the Chair – Modern Salon

FrontRow Monthly, FrontRow Monthly, Inc., 2012

Uniforms

Most beauty school students are required to wear a uniform. Some schools use their logo for the shirt portion of the uniform, and some schools choose not to place the name of the school onto the uniforms. The student's uniform is very much like a pair of scrubs that are used in the medical field.

Taking School Seriously

You can attend a beauty school to be a part of something great, or you can just be there to take up space. As many of my classmates were either outside smoking, taking long lunches, or not coming at all to class at all, I was trying my best to take everything in and really make something of this opportunity. We all have the choice to waste time in class or benefit from what we are learning, even if what we are studying seems to be of no use to us at the time. It is really up to each of us to go for it and accomplish what we are meant to do. It is my belief that God has given all of us many gifts, and we just need to make the best use of them in our careers.

Beauty school, for me, was a way for me to become someone unique, and to establish who I was becoming as a young adult. My education helped me to mature and grow as an individual in the nine months that I spent in the classroom. As I look back on that great experience, I think how blessed and fortunate I was to be so aware of what I wanted from life. The instruction that I received in beauty school gave me the confidence in life to be the person I am today. As in any profession, you need to feel it, love it, and really want it, to be able to take it to the next level.

Some of the challenges you may face as a cosmetology student will be encountered as you learn the biological side of cosmetology. In short, you will be required to learn the science behind the beauty industry. You will study, not only hair, but skin and nail analysis. You will learn to assess and evaluate what your future clients will need to properly care for their hair, skin and nails, and you will make valuable recommendations and suggestions to them based on what you learn during these courses. The good or bad condition of a client's hair, nails, and skin are often an indication of the state of their health, diet, and lifestyle. You will learn what illnesses, medications, or chemicals will affect the hair, skin, and nails. Also, if you are considering the field of cosmetology, remember that you will not just study how to cut and style hair, but you will also be introduced to makeup application, and you will learn how to teach clients how to take care of all of their beauty needs.

Taking a *Leap of Faith*

Early in my career, my main focus was to work in a salon and learn all the different aspects of the industry. Along the way, I got married to my high-school sweetheart and had two beautiful children. My focus shifted to my family for several years, but I stayed true to myself for the passion that was in me. My second child was getting ready to start school and I knew I would have more time to pursue some interests. This amazing door opened up for me to have my own salon, and I was so excited to welcome that challenge. We all need to take chances, because if the decision is a good one, great opportunities will be waiting for us. There are times in all of our lives when we must reach out for those opportunities. I'll never forget that day the sign went up in front of my first hair salon with my name on it! You just cannot believe the feeling you have when you realize that this is what you have been preparing for years, and you know you are on your way to success.

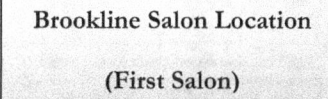

Brookline Salon Location

(First Salon)

Downtown Salon Location

(Second Salon)

When you are working as a hairstylist (cosmetologist), you can meet so many amazing people. The clients and your coworkers, whom you will work with over the years, become an extension of your own family in many ways. You meet people from all walks of life in a hair salon. You will build relationships and form friendships with your clients. Because you will see your clients on a regular basis, you will get to know each other well, and you will share stories about your lives. From the weddings, to the births, to the funerals, you will laugh and cry. We as hairstylists are a comfort to our clients when they have hard times, and a support to them when they are planning for special events. As a stylist, you will play an important role in completing a client's look for their photographs for an upcoming graduation, prom, or wedding. We also can relate to them and help them get through a crisis by improving their outward appearance.   They can regain a sense of well-being and you can see them lift up again, inside and out.

In this business, you have clients who are always late, always early, or always in a hurry, or the ones who want to stay all day. There are clients who won't change their style, ones who want something new each time, ones who ask the same questions every time you see them, or the ones who won't talk at all. Whether the clients are loud or quiet, young or mature, they are your clients. Your client is the person who makes your passion and dreams stay alive. Without them, you would not have a business. Do not take your clients for granted. Always show respect and calmness when working with your clients. Give 100% of your time and talents when working with your client, and never lose sight of the importance of a great stylist/client relationship. In order to keep your business successful, you must always keep educating yourself and recharging your batteries. Keep the desire alive, and set goals and work towards them.

Classic Hairstyles

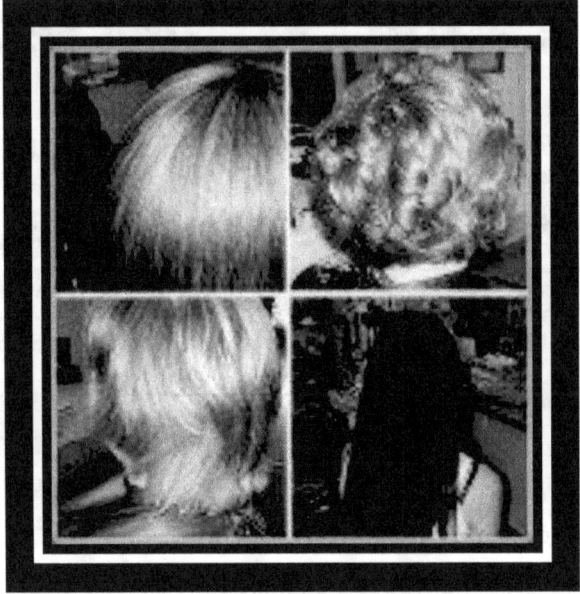

Before and After Makeovers

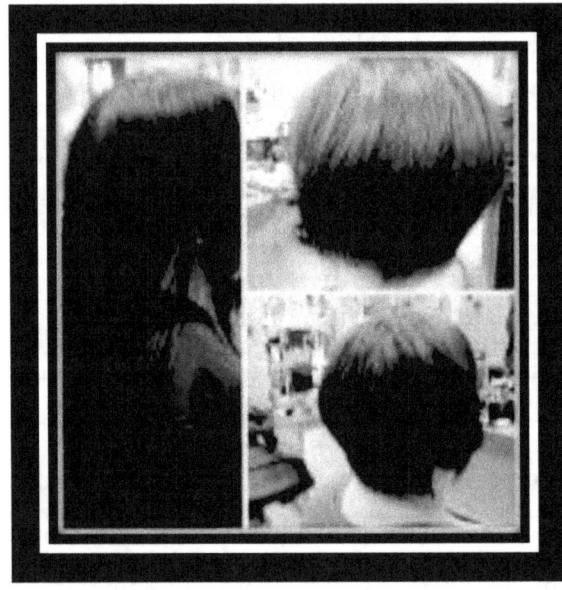 

Chapter 3

Salon Workshop

1. The Cutting Edge
2. Corrective Color
3. Hair Myths and Truths

1. The Cutting Edge. Before cutting, things to remember:

1. Natural movement of the hair. How does it fall? What shape does it take naturally?

2. Weight. Take in to consideration the density of the hair. Feel it, move it around, fine, medium, or coarse, then you will know to take away weight or build weight or if you just need to blend weight.

3. Head and facial shape. Check the bone structure and features. By doing this you can now give the best cut for that client.

4. Hair Maintenance at Home. A lot of stylists forget this. How will the client style their hair at home? Some clients cannot do their own hair or they find caring for their hair to be a challenge. Make sure you are giving them the best tips for maintaining their style at home.

5. Technique. There are many different techniques to create! You must learn, learn, and learn! Never stop educating yourself; we are part of a changing industry. One thing is for sure though, you need to have the basics first and then you have the foundation to create the perfect masterpiece. Your potential is endless.

Cutting Techniques and Texture

- **Solid lines -** more blunt cut/the classic bob
- **Light layering -** short at the crown and longer at the perimeter gives you a fuller layered look on top, and softer layers at the bottom
- **Heavy layering -** creates fullness and keeps length to create more weight, shorter to longer
- **Uniform -** the hair is equal lengths throughout the style to enhance a more uniform look

- **Graduated -** hair at the nape is shorter and the crown is longer, this gives you a graduated result with more weight at the mid to top area
- **Texture -** changing the surface of the cut
- **Thinning -** remove bulk, create a lighter movement within the structure of the design, this will give you a more blended finish
- **Notching -** produce strong to mild texture in the hair, can be used to create softer, more defined styles
- **Perming for texture -** style support waves, creates fullness, fatness in the hair without all the curl. This gives you more control and not frizz and curl.

2. **Corrective color.**

- **Consult.** A gentle consultation is recommended. Remember to focus on the solution to the problem. You need to listen carefully to the client to understand all of the details.

- **Plan of action.** You must have a beginning and ending goal. A roadmap to start a successful result. Make sure you are in agreement with the client. Let the client know it may take a few times to see the best results. Never promise unrealistic hairstyle results to your client. Explain that their desired result may take several color applications to achieve. It is best to be honest at the beginning of the process to avoid any disappointment or high expectations for instantaneous results.

- **Too much brass or orange.** This problem occurs when you have not lifted to the proper stage. When trying to lift too high, color will only lift so much. You need to neutralize the warmth rather than trying to continue to lift more. Use a formula to cancel out the warmth for a much softer tone. Also a lower developer will give you more control.

- **Too much dark.** When dealing with too much dark in the hair, it is best to clarify the hair first. Instead of going all over and decolorizing the hair, apply a lot of thin highlights to control the process for even distribution and more blended results. Process to a gold stage and then apply a demi-permanent gloss to a natural shade. You want to use a low developer to keep the hair in good condition.

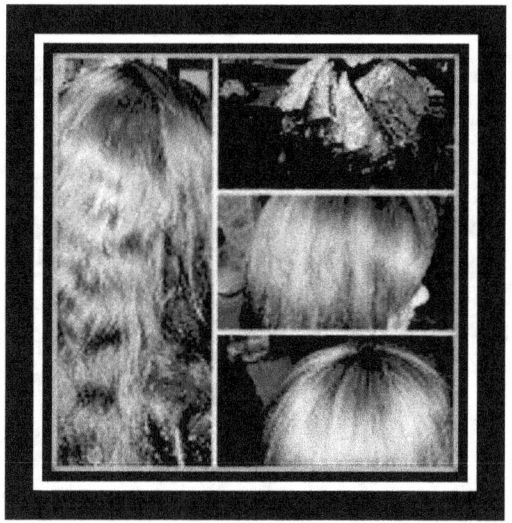

Color Class 101

Steps to Formulate:

1. Determine the client's natural level
2. Evaluate the client's desired level and tones
3. Factor in the clients residual pigment contribution (RPC)
4. Estimate or gauge the tone value desired
5. Measure the proper strength developer

Foil Placement

Sections

- Decide on a design that you want to achieve
- Section out to desired design and clip
- Always keep straight lines and clip to secure the hair
- Neat and clean – clean lines and separation are very important in foil placement

Placement

- Create your subsection and neatly comb out and clip unwanted section
- Place point of comb near scalp, pick up selected strands, and smooth out hair
- Weave or slice close to scalp (do not dip) to prevent banding, slipping, bleeding
- Use tail of comb to slide foil against scalp to stabilize with index finger and thumb

Ombre Technique

Color Placement

- Begin placing loaded color brush one inch away from the lid of the foil, moving through the ends. Use the side of the brush in short, choppy, strokes for natural looking results called, *feathering*. Fold the foil up to cover the strands placing the bottom edge of the foil to the base of parting, fold again. Do not press on middle, crease the sides for support.

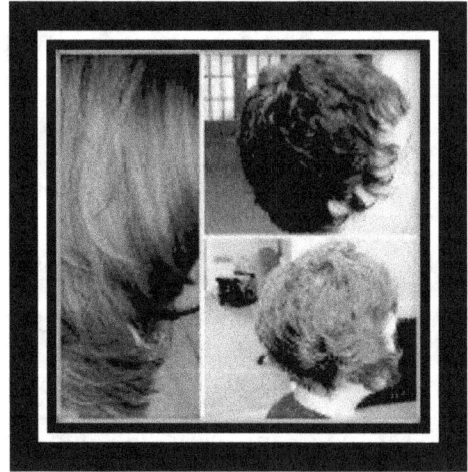

- **Color -** creates an illusion, gives you the appearance of change, and enhances the total value of the hair color. This will give you volume and increase texture as well as create shine and vibrancy.

3.   **Hair Myths and Truths.**

True or False:

Frequent shampooing will make your hair fall out.
False - Balding or thinning hair is usually genetic or related to a health issue. A clean scalp will help build up from occurring and makes the hair and scalp look and feel healthy. A stress or mineral imbalance may cause temporary hair loss, not frequent shampooing.

Going a few shades lighter as you get older will soften your look.
True - There is no need to go lighter than that.

All About You...

What makes you want to be a stylist? _____

What would you say are your worst fears? _____

What is the best advice you ever got? _____

What are your greatest accomplishments? _____

How do you rate yourself? _____

What inspires you? _____

Monday Workshops at Jacqueline's Salon

No matter how many years you may have worked in the salon industry, you must continue to educate yourself and practice new ideas.

Chapter 4
A New You

Attitude. I have worked with many different stylists in this industry and one thing that I have learned is that attitude is one of the main focus points in our career. In my own salon, I have always been able to tell which employees will be the ones who will take things seriously. I remember a time when we were getting ready to kick off a theme party at the salon. Everyone was so excited, except for one employee who couldn't care less. She had no desire, no drive, and no ambition. For me, that just seems like a waste of time and talents. This employee complained constantly and tried to bring the rest of us down with her poor attitude. We could have let her weigh us down, but instead we let our excitement and enthusiasm shine through until it was contagious. Before you knew it she was getting involved and participating in the event. You must stand up for yourself and not let those individuals with bad attitudes get in your way. Remember, you are on this beautiful road to success. How can you keep a good attitude?

> ## Attitude

Take Care of Yourself. What gives you your will power? Where do find your strength? We all need to keep ourselves feeling good. Get plenty of rest and keep yourself in a healthy state. Try to maintain a good diet when you are in this profession. In the salon, we tend to eat on the go, because we are focused on the timing of the client's appointments. Try and give yourself that extra time between appointments. You should sit and have your lunch at work, take a little break to rest your tired feet and legs from standing all day. Step outside for some fresh air, take some deep breaths. You need that time in the day to regroup, refocus, and recharge your batteries.

Faith. How do I begin? My faith has brought me to where I am today. I feel like I am in a good place, and I know I could never have gotten anywhere in life without my faith. Faith is what you believe in the deepest part of your soul. Your spirit is yours, and no one can take it from you. You feel it, you own it. Be strong within yourself, stay humble and calm. Let your faith guide you and all things are possible. If you pray and have faith, it is my belief that God will answer when the time is right. I know that not everyone has religious faith in his or her lives, but for me, faith has been behind every success that I have ever had in my life. I wish that everyone could experience the joy that faith has brought to me. These are my beliefs, but if you have the will, desire, and faith in yourself, you will succeed.

Positive Outlook. Wow, this is a feeling that can go up and down. You are moving along smoothly when issues and problems arise, and now you feel like things are not going as planned. Your great day can soon turn hectic really quickly. Your positive attitude can turn negative really fast. Take a step back and look at the real picture. See it for what it is. Okay, so those extensions didn't go as planned, or that haircut you gave that new client didn't work out for her. Look at the situation and make it better. Give the client options. Show the client how to take care of their new look at home. The client may just need time to get used to the new style. Do everything you can to make your client feel beautiful and turn this negative back in to a positive. It is the manner in which we manage these mishaps that make us better at our craft. It helps us to grow. Always see the good in every situation. When thing do not go according to the plan, review what you learned from the experience in order to prevent the mistake from occurring again.

Never give up. I remember when I was just starting to learn how to mix and apply hair color. At times, it was like I was trying to understand a different language. I learned many lessons from my experience of cutting and coloring my brother's friend's hair. Tom wanted me to lighten his hair, so I got the product, applied it, and all of the sudden his hair looked orange. I got really scared because I wasn't sure how to fix it. We rinsed it off, but needless to say he looked ridiculous. He went to the park after to play basketball with my brother and his other friends, and they just had a blast calling him names like *carrot top, orange head,* and all kinds of other things. He was the joke of the day. I tried to fix it, but it only got worse. I had to shave his head, and you can only imagine the comments he received. I could have said, *I will never try color again,* but I put that disaster behind me. I was even more determined to figure out what I was doing wrong. Today, I love applying color. It's my favorite part of cosmetology, and I took it on full force in my salon. You can be creative and show your many different techniques with color. I am glad that I never gave up on learning color application. I had to take on the challenge and not let it defeat me. If I did not accept that challenge, I would not be the colorist I am today. Incidentally, in spite of the color mishap, Tom continued to be one of my clients for several years.

Round – you need a textured bob with lots of layers help to narrow a round face, or a blunt cut bob that slims the face, with face-framing angles

Square – layered and soft curls. These wavy layers work well to frame and soften a square face.

Triangular – face framing curls or long fluffy layers. Shoulder length hair adds softness to the face.

Long face – classic bob, middle length bob cut to the jaw with a full bang.

Oval – the perfect facial shape can wear just about anything.

Heart – fullness around the chin area and smooth behind the ear – soft bang and height on top

Visualize

Dress:
ngth above knee
iris made flower with middle stones
ress in a lace like look knit
ack to drape / low cut back
houlder strap in crystal stone
Dress Lined

Sample Dress In White
Flower Light Pink Color

Gown in White
White fur

matching
fur Stole

fur neckline

Rhinestones
on Bodice
and waist

Rhinestone
Straps on
shoulders

Long gloves
with fur
accent

* Skirt with
slit in front
* Skirt Elegant
Knit
Lined

Gown - Full skirt to floor

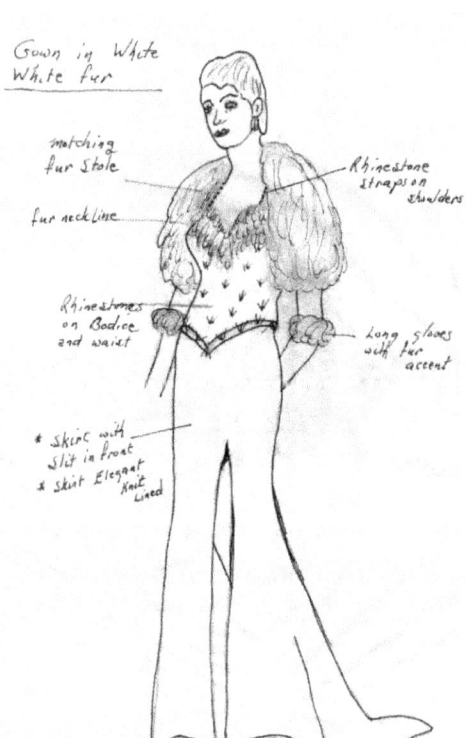

Fashion and Hair Design Blend to Complete the Package

Debi Weiss, Fashion and Designer Gallery Intl
Fashion and Designer Gallery Intl

Chapter 5

Business Management 101

1. **Work Smarter, Not Harder**

2. **Business Growth – Ten Tips for Business Growth.**

3. **Employer - Employee**

4. **Financial Gain / Marketing – Part I and Part II**

5. **Social Media / Marketing**

1. **Work Smarter, Not Harder**

Don't take on too much at once. Learn to say no if things are too busy in life. Ask yourself what is most important. Don't procrastinate, and try and get in the habit of doing a certain amount of work each day. There is always tomorrow! Eventually, you will have your daily regime in order.

2. **Business Growth – Ten Tips for Business Growth**

It is crucial that you choose a good location for your business. You will want to make sure that your salon is in a thriving business district with a high traffic flow and access to parking for your clients.

Business growth takes time, and it does not happen overnight.

Steps to get you in line with reality:

1. Understand the meaning of patience
2. Learn to be persistent
3. Take care of the clients first
4. Be refreshing and new
5. Don't worry about competition – be the competition
6. Do your own thing, be your own person
7. Don't sweat the small stuff
8. Be pleasant – smile, have fun along the way
9. Educate and learn
10. Socialize – network, get out there, and let people know who you are

Growth

3. Employer – Employee

Policy and Procedures Manual

It is essential that you provide a policy and procedure manual for your employees so that you can outline the rules and regulations that they will need to follow when they are working in your salon. You should ask your employees to sign an agreement that states that they have read the manual, and that they fully understand what is expected of them. Ask them if they have any questions to prevent any misinterpretations of the policies.

Respect and Loyalty

One thing I have learned over these years is that no matter what side you are on, if you are an employee or an employer (and this goes for any business), you must have respect for one another. When I started in this industry I worked for two barbers. You can really learn a lot form barbers. One was a woman and the other was a man. They taught me so much about haircutting for men. They both had successful businesses, and they really gave me a great start. I wanted to do a good job, be on time, and be productive when I was there. We all have to start at the bottom and work up. Things don't happen overnight. Respect your employer. The barbers gave me a job, so I wanted to do well for them. We need to appreciate any job offer. This job was a stepping stone for me, and I wanted to learn all that I could about the business. You may just be a shampoo girl right now, and that is great. It is the beginning of something more to come. You need to get the experience first in order to prove yourself. We all have a lot to learn. There are people who do not view hairdressing as a real career, but in reality this industry is in a very powerful position. We are an important part of the fashion industry. We start trends. We make all those models and celebrities look their best. We also educate the general population on how to create these looks. Without us, they would not have the confidence or the look for that photo shoot or print advertisement. We deserve to be proud and feel good about this path that we have chosen. When you are out there working, understand your employer and get to know what type of salon that you are working in. Discover ways in which you can work with your employer to be successful.

I do know that in this business it does take time to build a clientele. I wouldn't relocate too often because clients do not want to follow you three, four, or five times, even if they love what you do. Try and find a salon that fits you and one you feel comfortable in so that you do not have to keep reinventing your business. Don't get me wrong, sometimes it takes a while to find a salon that you can call home. Just be reasonable and really think it through when choosing the right one. Salons may have different ways of doing business, but one thing is for sure, we all need many clients to maintain a successful business. Also, we need a nice working environment with great employee and employer team work. As an employer, I really appreciate all that my team does to improve Jacqueline's Salon. In return, the employee sees their value in being a part of a team.

As an employee, show respect and be willing to go that extra mile. Strive to be on time, and if you need to stay late every once in a while, do it. Avoid expressing complaints in the salon, and keep gossip out of the workplace. Be a good coworker and treat the clients well.

Gracefully Leaving Your Place of Employment

If you are asked to leave a position, be polite and professional. If things don't work out, remember they gave you that opportunity. Give the respect back and make it right when it is time to move on.

If it is your decision to leave your place of employment, you should give a two-week notice and leave on good terms. Express your gratitude to your employer for giving you the opportunity to work for them. If you would ever want to return to this place of business in the future, you would most likely be welcomed back, if you left on good terms.

Responsibilities of an Employer

Do everything to help the employees be successful. Give the employee a great workplace to be a part of. Realize that employees may come and go but stick to your mission and values and you will be rewarded. Do not take it personally if an employee decides to take another position.

As an employer, there may be times when you must release an employee, and it is important to show them respect and encouragement during this stressful and uncomfortable circumstance. If it is time for someone to move on, hopefully, they will give you the chance to wish them well. Keep your head up and keep moving forward. Building a team takes hard work and dedication.

Death of a Co-worker

It is extremely difficult to lose a good employee if they decide to relocate to another salon. However, you never imagine that one of your employees will pass away, and nothing can prepare you for their loss when this occurs.

My employee, Gail, was a good friend and a good hairstylist. After working in my Brookline salon for seven years, Gail had steadily built up her clientele over this period of time. When I received the phone call that she had died suddenly, I had the painful task of contacting each of her clients with the devastating news. Her friendships with her coworkers and clients went back many years. Clients have a close relationship with their hairdresser, and Gail's clients found the shocking news to be very hard to accept. All of us in the salon wanted to honor Gail. Since Gail was such a great football fan, we all dressed in black and gold and decorated her station with all sorts of football paraphernalia in the weeks that followed her death. She would have loved that, and what a way to celebrate her life! Most of Gail's clients continued to come to the Brookline salon, and we were able to accommodate them and retain them as clients. This is where working together as a team really pays off. Gail's clients needed to make an abrupt decision about whether to continue to come to our salon or go elsewhere. As a team, we respectfully offered our services to them. As an employer, you do not want to lose clients for any reason, and finding solutions in even the hardest of times, is what makes your salon stand out from the rest. I was very proud of my team for the wonderful job that we all did even when we were heartbroken.

Tip: Always keep good records for your client's formulas and all of their information in case of emergency.

Hair Shows and Conventions – Employee Education

A hair show is something most of you probably have experienced or should experience. How exciting a weekend away with coworkers can be as we continue our education to become better stylists (well, that only applies to most of us). On the other hand, there are some who look at it as a weekend of partying. They start drinking on the way to the event and continue to drink for the next two days. I would hear people say, *New techniques, what's that? Get me to the bar for a margarita!* It is nice to have a good time and let your hair down, and I really do like to dance and have fun, but some balance is always a good thing. Hair shows are really a lot of excitement. The demonstrations provide fresh new ideas for you to take back to your salon and clients. Use the time at a hair show to network and hear stories that you can relate to. For example, there are times when a client wants to look like that certain celebrity, and you know there is no way that is going to happen. You need to tactfully explain that you can give them some variation of that look. As a hairstylist, you are bound to hear at some point, *I just cut my hair and messed it up, and can you fix it? But, don't take much off.* While you are assessing the damage, you know you will need to cut about three inches off to make it look even. The client will expect you to perform a miracle without taking off any length. You will need to be honest with them and learn to reassure them that you will do your best to give them a great style that will regrow nicely. Hair shows can shed light on important tips to pass onto your clients, and they are a way to connect and recharge your batteries. Try not to drink and dance on the bar too much so you can actually learn something while still having a good time!

Hard work will pay off!

| Casino Night |
| Theme |

4. Financial Gain / Marketing – Part I

Financial Gain and Preparing for *Rainy Days*

Your revenue can fluctuate, so it will be important for you to be prepared for the slower times in your business. Keep a log of months so that you can predict which months are leaner and which months are profitable. Organize your budget so you don't get too far behind on incoming bills. For those periods of time where you have fewer clients, you will need to learn to reduce your spending and inventory. Be sure to order only what you need not what you want. Salon promotions will bring additional customers through your door. You can find creative ways to make the slower months more profitable by building a plan of action that will help you get through these times and produce more for your bottom line.

Give thanks to your new clients by sending them a thank you card and a coupon. This lets the client know how much you appreciate their business.

- Explain your referral program, when they refer people to you, they will receive 10% off of their next visit

- Birthday celebration. We now will give gift certificates on a flyer for them to bring in a friend to help them celebrate

- Rebook them. Every client who rebooks on the spot gets an entry form for a drawing for a special prize of the month

- Tell and sell. Explain the products and what the client needs. Tempt and treat them by showing how the product works.

Once you are a professional hair stylist, and you must learn to combine product sales with client education.

Financial Gain / Marketing Part II – Combining Sales with Product Education

1. Selling products and services is a skill.
   - Can be learned, practiced, and achieved
   - Become familiar with your products
   - Exposure, education, experience

2. Teaching the client how your products and services will best suit their needs
   - Provide best product for a client's needs
   - Natural extension of quality services

3. Help your client to learn how to achieve their look at home.
   - Able to recreate the look the next day
   - Promote one or two items for your client to use at home.
   - Best items for the look they have and the problem they need solved

Goal: The goal is to challenge yourself by asking clients what problems they are having. Listen to their response, and suggest certain products or services to meet their needs.

 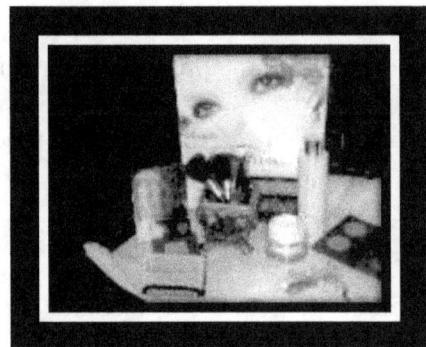

Salon Potential for Growth (Fill in the Work Sheet)

Active base: _____

Frequency of visit: _____

Average ticket: _____

New clients per month: _____

New client retention: _____

5. Social Media / Marketing

Social media is a whole new world, and this new technology will help you to succeed. Websites, such as: *Google, Facebook, Twitter*, are visited by your customers, and it would be wise for you to create your own website to communicate with them. Marketing your business is going to be a long term commitment. If you are not computer savvy, find someone who can to take on this role for your business. There are amazing developments in social media to help your salon succeed. Many new challenges and opportunities are waiting for you so get on board and let the social media trend take your salon to the next level.

Let the social media help you to make new friends or connect with old ones. Social media can help you to gain more profit for your bottom line. Offer salon promotions online to increase your website traffic. When you are creating your web page, you should keep in mind who you want to target and design your website to appeal to those in your target group.

At the end of the day, you want to build your brand. You *are* your brand, so as you are marketing your services and getting involved in social media, keep in mind all of the opportunities you have for gaining traffic flow into your place of business. Collect e-mail data from new clients, and potential clients. You can then send out an email blast to customers for monthly promotions.

Social media can become a great way to spread the word about your brand and let people know what your business has to offer to the community. Customize your e-mail messages to target specific groups of people and you can create new and exciting ideas to use all year long. It is important to build trust with the people with whom you are networking. Use social media as a tool to secure your growing business. Promote yourself and end up with more profit, more clients, and much more exposure.

New Avenues

Think outside the salon. You don't have to just stand behind the chair all day to be successful. Explore different aspects of your industry and blend them with your salon services. Use your full cosmetology, fashion, and beauty background to expand your business. An online boutique can be a great way to sell your products, especially if you don't have a lot of product space inside your salon.

Are you interested in an online boutique in your salon? Please email me at Jhob2@aol.com. I can help you arrange this for your salon. A great way to enhance your salon is through the sales of Fluhme cosmetics! My customers really enjoy this line of high-quality makeup and accessories.

Business Management 102

1. **Balance**
2. **Retain and Create New Clients**
3. **What Are Clients Really Thinking?**
4. **Up Front and Personal**
5. **Different Looks, Different Folks**
6. **Helping Clients to Adjust to Adverse Situations**
7. **Inspiration**
8. **Our Clients' Self-Esteem**
9. **Practice – Practice – Practice**

1. **Balance**

How do we achieve balance with work, family, friends, and life? First you must realize that you can't do it all, or be in fifteen places at once. You need to prioritize, have patience, and be willing to compromise. You must divide your time. Give yourself some breathing room. Make time for yourself even if it's just to take a few minutes to have a beverage, to read, or to take a quick walk outside.

2. **Retain and Create New Clients**

    *   Remember to always treat clients with respect, give them a place to feel at home. Make yourself available, and have a set schedule so they become familiar with your days and times. Have some variety with days and evenings.

    *   Word of mouth - once you give a great salon experience to a client, that client will be more than happy to spread the word.

    *   Never take you clients for granted, always treat them like it was the first time they walked in your door. Clients come to you for the fabulous work you do, for the way they are treated, and for the atmosphere. Always give 110%, as my father would say!!

Balance

What are Clients Really Thinking?

Take some time to get to know your clients. A few clients may not be willing to share much about their personal life, but most will converse with you after the first consultation and a few appointments. You will learn if they are employed, if they are married or single, if they have children, and what interests or hobbies they have. You have to determine if they have the means to keep up with your salon services, and whether they will be a regular client, a client who comes every six months, or a yearly client. You need to evaluate what services will meet their individual needs. Also, as you learn what types of products they use and how they style their hair at home, you will learn the different products that you can offer to them to create their look at home. Once you understand the needs of your customers, you will see what fits their budget, habits, and lifestyle. Over time, you will build a successful stylist/client relationship.

3. **Up Front and Personal**

Clients will respect your honesty, when they are seeking your professional opinion. Give them straight answers. You will need to determine what is best for their hair texture, face shape, and bone structure. Listen carefully to their requests so that you can give them an appropriate answer.

Different Looks, Different Folks

What types of clients are you expecting to encounter? Are you the versatile hairstylist or one who will only specialize in one or two things? You should very clear when communicating with your clients about the services that you can or cannot provide. Everyone is different and unique in their own way. You never know who will come into your salon, so be prepared for a variety of hair textures and types.

4. Helping Clients to Adjust to Adverse Situations

When times are tough for clients, learn to be willing to suggest ways to get them through difficult times.

Example 1: A full head of hair has now become very fine. Give them hope, and suggest the right product or service for scalp treatments, or maybe a new cut to give lift and volume.

Example 2: Your client has lost her job. Discuss different ways to help her maintain her hair color. She does not want to have grey hair. You could forego the highlights and suggest that she use color only. Or if things are really bad, she can request the base color and you can still do the highlights. As a last resort, you could privately offer her a temporary discount for your services. She will appreciate the help and stay loyal to you in the long run.

7. Inspiration

We all have been inspired at one time or another to pursue an education, apply for a certain job, take up a hobby, or to travel to places of interest. It is our job as the professional stylist is to stay inspired and motivated about improving the appearance of our clients. Our clients often come to us for advice about trying new styles, and they need our encouragement to help them to make the change in their style.

What inspires you? Are you attracted to nature, art forms, fabrics, or fashion designing? Stay in touch with what inspires you. Aspire to be inspired.

8. Our Clients' Self-Esteem

We boost our clients' self-esteem by providing them with great haircuts, color, styling, and makeup. Nothing feels better as a professional cosmetologist than to see the look on a client's face in the mirror when you have just completed a new look for them and they love it. Their whole face lights up (unless they don't love it, now that's a different story!). When you can see that they feel like a million bucks, you enjoy their reaction. Our goal is to give our clients confidence in themselves. It is rewarding to see a client who has a special glow from the inside out. If for some reason they don't like the new look, work on it until they do. Don't let them leave until they are happy with their new look.

9. Practice, Practice, Practice

Know that you will make mistakes and train yourself to do better next time. Once you realize that you are not alone, and that we have all made mistakes, you can achieve so much more. Learn from any errors that you do make and try to prevent them from happening in the future. Never let failure defeat you! Give yourself a pat on the back, and begin to move in the right direction. Stay focused and set goals. You will succeed one step at a time.

This will be the place where you make a difference in people's lives.

Chapter 6

Imagine Your Future

1. **Issues in Life**
2. **Building Your Future**
3. **Remaining on Track and Staying Focused**
4. **Imagine and Inspire**
5. **Realize**
6. **Basic Training – For the salon and For Life**
7. **First Impression – Guide to Help With a Consultation**

1. Issues in Life

All of our lives are a mix of good and bad experiences. Depression due to the loss of a loved one, loss of a pet, loss of a job, divorce, or even loss of self-respect can prevent us from reaching our potential. Adversities can help to make us stronger, especially when we realize we cannot do this alone. A strong faith in God has helped me though trials, but whatever your beliefs may be, it is important to have faith in your talents, skills, and strengths. Refuse to let the negative issues rule or ruin your life.

Things are not always going to go how you plan. You will have a lot of trial and error. This is how you grow, learn, and succeed. It takes time to perfect something. Sometimes your business may be booming and other times business may be slower. We all get knocked down, but you need to get up again and avoid any situations that may keep your from moving forward. Work hard to do extraordinary things. For me, when times get tough I just find something positive to focus on, and then I feel better and more productive.

2. Building Your Future

Stay on course. Remain humble and patient. This is a new stage in your life. Look forward to your future. You will have a strong sense of satisfaction when you realize how far you have come, and what great potential you have to go further. We are on a journey and life is one big road map. As you go from stage to stage, making it through the good times and the bad, dig deep down and find that one passion that keeps you motivated and let that force help you to reach your destination. Ask yourself, *What is my purpose?*

As I look back on the things in my own life, there have been many times where I wanted to throw in the towel, give up, stay in bed, and not face the world. Many times when you say, *I don't care*, realize that this is an important moment in your life. You have the choice to keep going on that dark road or you can make the turn to a beautiful new open road that will lead you to success, happiness, and great rewards in your life. Don't look back, look ahead. We all need to have challenges because they get our blood flowing and gives us a reason to exist. Challenges and fears do keep us on our toes, and we need to face them and not let them cripple us. At times, I am afraid to drive the on the highway, and I get nervous and make every excuse not to go, but I just put on my seat belt, say a prayer, (put on the radio station, K-Love, to relax me), and I am on my way.

If I need to drive two hours to a hair show, I will do it. Don't let fear come between you and your goals. Ask yourself how you can prevent negative energy from destroying your aspirations.

3. Remaining on Track and Staying Focused

Accept the fact that you are who you are. You do not have to continue to beat yourself up for mistakes you have made, and you should not let your mistakes define you. Put the past behind you and move forward because this will give you strength to learn who you are and how important it is to believe in yourself.

4. Imagine and Inspire.

I always try to imagine how much better life can be if I surround myself with greatness. Life in so much more than we see sometimes. Imagine all the wonderful doors that God will open, if you believe. As hairdressers, we do inspire with our creativity, our dedication, and our desire to make things better. We help our clients to feel beautiful by pampering them and showing them respect. We listen to our clients, and we share our stories with them. That is the beauty of this industry. We inspire, mentor, educate, share, and become great friends with our clients. We are fortunate to be a part of something so fulfilling. Be proud of what you do. No one else can really say that they make people feel beautiful inside and out in quite the same way as we do in this profession.

Imagine

5. Realize

- **Realize** who you are, and **realize** that there is always room for improvement.
- **Realize** your talents.

- **Realize** your creativity.
- **Realize** that you can do this.
- **Realize** what is in store for you.

Reach for your goals by taking one step at a time. Stay motivated by the challenge and keep your eyes open for all of the opportunities that will come your way.

6. Basic Training – For the salon and For Life

Training takes practice, commitment, and confidence. If you learn to master your craft, it will lead you to great success in the salon. Absorb all the knowledge that you can, and still have fun along the way! Learn, learn, and learn!

7. First Impression – Guide to Help With a Consultation

You should always develop a routine that you plan to follow with each client. This will give the client a feeling of security and they will learn to trust your opinion.

1. Always welcome the client in to your salon and have them fill out a profile questionnaire
2. Offer coffee, tea, or water
3. Introduce yourself once they reach your chair
4. A consultation is so important. You need to have a plan on what services the client expects.
5. Look at their hair - texture, density, color, condition. Plan accordingly.
6. Ask questions, how do they style their hair? What products do they use? What are they comfortable with?
7. Listen to your client. It is very important that you and the client agree upon the service.
8. Give your suggestions.
9. Get a game plan.
10. Execute the plan start to finish.

Chapter 7

Professionalism

1. **Presentation – Front Desk Associate**

2. **Goals**

3. **Biggest Challenge**

1. **Presentation - Front Desk Associate**

It is important to discuss the responsibilities that are given to your front desk associate. An efficient front desk associate is essential to your business growth. When you give the front desk associate the job of greeting and welcoming clients to your place of business this associate needs to be well informed and educated about all of the salon procedures. This will give the front desk associate a purpose beyond just answering the phone. When you add this value to this position, you will find that your front desk associate will help with client retention, product sales, and generate revenue simply by discussing the various services that your salon offers to the clients. It will be beneficial to train front desk help to be aware of promotions for clients, how to preschedule appointments, and how to cross-refer services from one stylist to another. All of these front desk responsibilities should never be taken out of the business manual for they are crucial to maintaining relationships with your client base. When you are hiring front desk personnel, be sure to look for someone who gives a great first impression as they welcome your clients to your salon. They are the first person to meet and greet your guests.

From the minute a client walks in the salon, as a salon owner, you must:
- Be enthusiastic
- Learn what you can about your clients
- Understand their needs
- Learn about their lifestyle, and ask them which products they use.
- Learn how they style their hair, make up, etc.
- Teach them how to maintain their hairstyle.
- Complete new client forms when your new client arrives.

- Schedule your client's next appointment before they leave the salon, and give them your business card, a salon brochure, and a complimentary bag of product samples
- Conduct yourself professionally, by the way you speak, look, and express your body language

2. Goals

Tally and Goal Sheet

Set a goal for total clients, services, and retail. Keep track of your totals.

Month _____	Week 1	Week 2	Week 3	Week 4
Total Clients				
Service(s)				
Retail				
Grand Total				

3. **Biggest challenge**

   1. Getting out of our comfort zone

   2. Retailing

   3. Up-Selling

   4. Staying motivated and interested

   5. Rebooking and retaining

   6. Realize that we work for our clients, and we should never take them for granted.

(Fill in your own ideas below.)

   7. _____

   8. _____

   9. _____

   10. _____

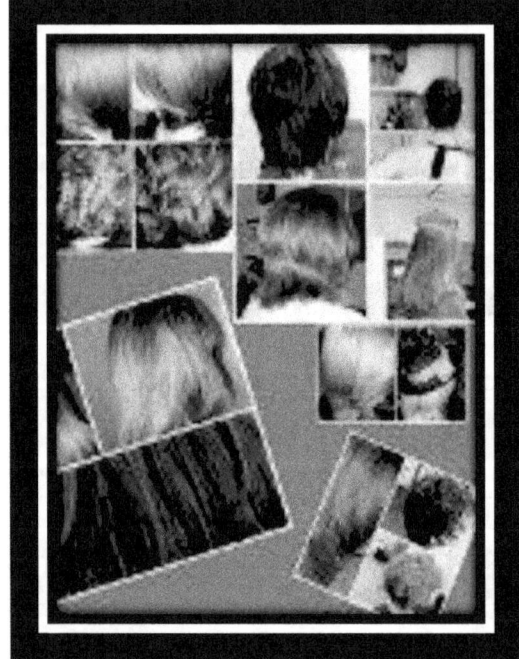

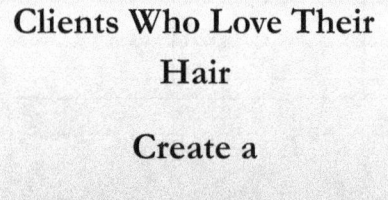

Clients Who Love Their Hair

Create a

"Look Book"

Classic Style

Chapter 8

Inspiration

What's your story?

- What inspired you to join the beauty world? _____

- Describe yourself in one word._____

- What are your career goals? _____

- How can you become a better coworker? _____

- How can you increase your client base and retail sales? _____

Inspiration Bulletin Board

Candles are delightful.

The inspiration from a candle as it burns and the light that it reflects stirs up emotions inside of us. Candles that have different textures and multiple colors and fragrances give you the fresh feeling of nature and growth. Candle displays add warmth to your salon environment, and candle sales can boost revenue in your salon.

Imagine a garden full of fragrance and beautiful color.

Flowers:

The soft petals and elegant smooth texture of flowers are nature at its very best. When you look at a beautiful flower it gives you a sense of calmness and relaxation. I get so inspired when I see the floral shades bounce off of each other in perfect harmony. I carry this same appreciation of color over to my work with hair color. I love to blend the subtle colors found in nature with brighter shades to create a natural look for the customer. Using shades within the same family creates an artistic look that is young and fresh. You can be as creative as you want to be with many different colors. All of us are like flowers just waiting to bloom. As you are developing your skills in the salon, you will find your talents unfolding like the petals of a flower. As humans, we show our beauty in many different ways: through a smile, a helping hand, or a good deed. It is not just about the way you look. It is about who you are as a person!

Jacqueline's Beauty Tips:

Tip: Natural Essential Oils
What can they do for you? Lavender is calming, green tea and mint will re-energize, and jojoba is high in vitamin E and hydrating, which will also help any inflamed skin!

Tip: Blue Nails
They come from poor circulation. Eggshell nails happen when nails become too thin and separate from the nail bed. Bruised nails can come from careless filing. If you have any of these types, a bi-weekly manicure will help, but some may need a dermatologist to examine troubled skin and nails.

Tip: Take a Dip
Paraffin dips are the perfect way to relax! Stop in on your lunch break. Feel the difference in the softness of your hands and moisture your cuticles. This will help you grow beautiful and healthy nails.

Live, Laugh, Love

To live fully, laugh often, and to love genuinely is truly a great way of life. If you think about it, these three words that begin with "L" are so powerful. *Live* – we all walk around every day with our thoughts, our emotions, and our feelings swirling around inside of us. How you live your life is really a choice. You can choose to be happy, sad, kind, or mean. You can choose to follow your passion or choose to ignore or suppress it. Life give us so many choices, sometimes too many. We must figure out what is important, what really matters. What will help us be who we were meant to be? Inside your heart you know who you are and what your purpose it. Find it and hold on to it. Live your life well. *Laugh* – I love to laugh. Who doesn't? We need to be able to enjoy things and have a good time with coworkers, family, and friends. After a hard day at work, take a moment and unwind. Rest your brain and do something that makes you happy, something that will make you smile. It is good for the soul. Give yourself time every day to enjoy the beautiful things in life. Go to the park, see a funny movie, or read a good story. Whatever it is, laugh and smile. You look much more beautiful when you do. *Love* – Allow yourself to love others, and remember to love yourself in a healthy way. If you make good choices, and you know deep down that you are a good person, there is no stopping you to accomplish your dreams. It is important that you love the work that you do. Believe in what you create. When you give someone a fabulous haircut, or a stunning make up application, you did that. Have faith and confidence in yourself. Let love in and you will be overwhelmed with joy. Live, laugh, and love are three words that mean so much, and they are the heart and soul of our existence.

Chapter 9

Creating Your Own Collection

The Crystal Collection - Inspired by Fifteen Years in the Profession

The crystal collection was born out of a vision after working for fifteen years in the business. The traditional gift for a fifteen-year wedding anniversary is a piece of crystal. I looked at the shapes of different types of crystals, and compared them with different techniques of haircutting.

Creating a seasonal collection will show your creative side to your clients and will give them a better perspective on what you are presenting to them. When you find yourself inspired by colors and shapes, put a theme together. Organize your thoughts through the use of photographs and soon your portfolio will feature many examples of your styles and hair color shades. The collection allows you to use your creative and artistic designs to produce versatility, harmony, and inspiration.

- **CRYSTAL –** Crystal is a term used to describe a clear or transparent mineral or glass. A crystal can be faceted to reflect light.

- **GEOMETRICAL –** Geometrical refers to curved or straight lines that are used to create to make shapes.

- **SYMMETRIC –** Symmetry means that each half of an object is similar and/or equal to the other half.

- **TRANSPARENT –** An object is considered to be transparent or clear if it has the property of transmitting light without scattering the light.

Samples from
Jacqueline's Crystal Collection

Elegance   Romance

Fifteen-Year Anniversary

The Love Collection

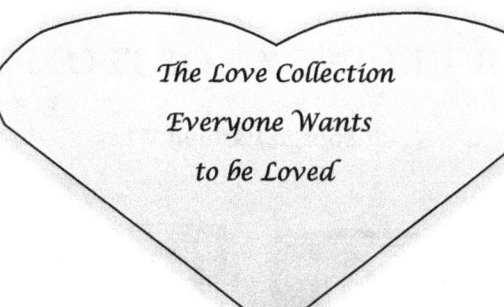

The Love Collection
Everyone Wants
to be Loved

The bridal industry inspired me to create the Love Collection.   The shapes, designs, and placement of one-process color, highlights, and low-lights are derived from the different styles of engagement rings. The *princess cut* was inspired from the idea that a bride should be a princess for the day. This cut is designed to enhance any of the love collection color techniques. This squared off look can be interchanged to be more edgy, romantic, or pop with bolder results. The *marquise cut* is created for a side part to enhance any style, and the *heart-shaped cut* is perfect for one length hair and heavy bangs. Hairstyles such as updos, and asymmetrical looks that can be accessorized with flowers, pearls, tiaras, and jeweled veils to create a regal look that is appropriate for this special day in a woman's life. I have many examples of these looks in my upcoming chapter on Wedding Planning. Your salon should offer a variety of traditional and trendy looks for your clients.

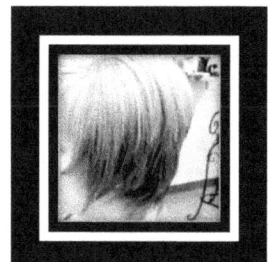

Short: Pop—bolder, spikier, shorter finish, pointed cut

Medium: Edgy—side part, textured, piece, point and razor

Long: Romantic—heavy bang. Softer, choppy and layered, fuller with more bounce

Chapter 10

BUILDING A PORTFOLIO

Pittsburgh Fashion Week
2012

Barry Felix, Jett Productions

Debi Weiss, Fashion and Designer Gallery Intl

 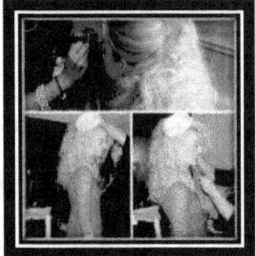

Backstage Preparations

This is Mia,

the Goddess of Growth

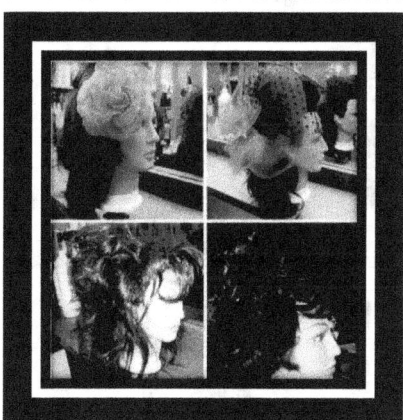

Community Scarecrow Contest – Autumn 2012

Vote for Dolly – Brookline's Most Stylish Scarecrow!

CONTEMPORARY

Editorial Magazine Photographs

Imagine and stay focused, and you could have your work in a magazine someday!

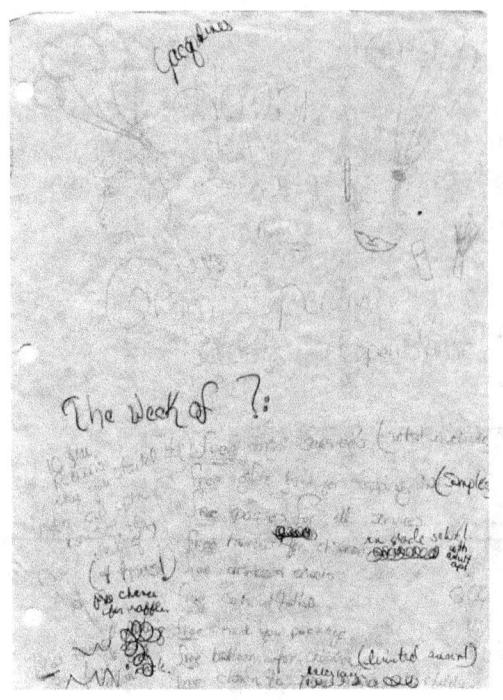 

A dream came true from these early ideas!

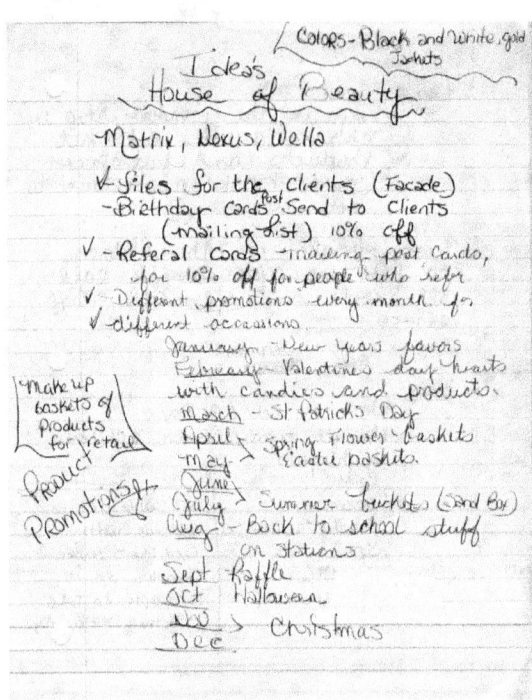

Humble Beginnings
I scribbled these notes of my dream of opening a salon back in 1988.
My first salon opened in 1994.

66

Chapter 11
Wedding Planning

Bridal Beginnings

When a future bride walks in to your salon or calls and asks questions concerning her wedding day, you need to be prepared for this special consultation. She will be excited, energized, and happy to talk to you, the beauty professional. She will need help with her plans for her look and will want to feel fabulous on that special day. It is your job to make sure that she has a wonderful experience from the moment that she first walks into your salon until the day that she is ready to walk down the aisle. This future bride will put all her trust in you. If you don't make a good first impression, she will move on to the next salon. Know what you are talking about. This is a great opportunity for you to grow your bridal business and also gain future clients for other everyday services.

1. **First thing is first…**
   - Find out the wedding date and time.
   - How many bridesmaids, flower girls, etc.?
   - Are you styling the mother of the bride and mother of the groom?

2. **Service they wish to have**
   - Hair, skincare, makeup, nails, extensions, products needed, packages, etc.

3. **Set up pre work**
   - Conditioning treatments, spa treatments, color/highlights, cuts, glosser, practice date, etc.

4. **Get all of the appointments scheduled and bring the bride an appointment card to mark her calendar.**
   - She will be busy so you need to keep her organized with a schedule.
   - Appointments should start a few months prior to the wedding date.

5. **Ok, so you know you are on the right path…**

   - Appointments are set

   - Make sure you have a count, services, a date, and a plan in place.

   - Make sure you double check appointment times and days to be correct and precise

   - Coordinate with nail technicians, stylists, massage therapists, and makeup artists so you can schedule the time blocks so that the day runs smoothly. You don't want to run late especially on the wedding day.

6. **Make sure you preorder any products needed. You should have a list together from your consultation.**

   - Hair products

   - Makeup, gloss, lipstick, etc.

   - Honeymoon products for the bride and groom

7. **Preparations have been completed, and now it is the big day:**

   - Have some light refreshments

   - Be on time

   - Set up early

   - Have irons hot, clips and bobby pins out, etc.

   - Have team meeting with staff to go over wedding request

   - Get a good night sleep because you will need it!

8. **The party begins: Here Comes the Bride**

   - Everyone is in place

   - You have done all of your prep work, now execute your talent.

   - Give 110%. It is the bride's regal moment; make her feel like a princess.

   - If you prepared yourself well, you will succeed.

9. **Wrap it Up.**

   - Always give the bride a little take home surprise. A product, gift certificate, candle, etc.

   - Give the bridal party a client bag with coupons, gift card

   - Retain them as future clients

10. **Customer Satisfaction = Customer Loyalty**

    - You want the bridal party to be thoroughly pleased with your work. They will share the news of their great salon experience with friends, relatives, and coworkers.

Flower Girl

Little Brides
First Communion Style

Chapter 12

Spa Treatments

The following promotions are ones that I have used over the years at Jacqueline's House of Beauty:

Party Goals and Procedures – Make sure:

- that clients relax and enjoy themselves.
- to rebook clients for future spa services.
- to focus on clients talk about the service you are doing – the benefits it has, products used, and that you recommend products.
- you and your staff have positive and upbeat attitudes.
- that you and your staff keep cell phones off. We need to attend to the clients and stay on time.
- stay focused and use your time wisely, by rotating between clients while they are under the dryer, with bags on hands, etc.

Don't panic, it all works out. Just keep to your schedule and have a plan – worry about your clients and your job. Everyone will do their part and it will all be great! Have fun!

Hot Oil Treatments

- Brush through hair
- Heat up oil with hot water, run bottle under hot water or place into bowl with hot water to heat
- Apply oil to scalp first and then go back to shaft and ends
- Massage scalp – do a relaxing massage for 5 minutes to entire head then comb or rake with fingers through shaft and ends
- Place bag and put under dryer for 5 to 10 minutes
- Rinse and shampoo with clarifying shampoo and then use clarifying rinse (conditioner)
- Towel dry, comb and style in to place with product. Place client under dryer to finish service.

Hand treatments

- Have client wash hands or sanitizer
- Use mango exfoliant and apply with brush on hands (use sanitizer after each client)
- Use bag, place overtop of hands and put mitts on for 5 to 10 minutes
- Remove mitts then place warm towel over hands to remove product
- Next use moisturizer and massage hands
- File a little to clean ends of nails
- Apply a mango oil to cuticles and run into nails for a shiny finish
- Polish is extra $5.00 offer only if you have time

Nail Fun

1. Healthy beautiful nails should always be your goal for each client.
2. Introduce nail art by trying new, fun designs.
3. Clean neat cuticles are the key to a healthy looking nail.
4. Decals make nail art easy and fun (bigger ticket)
5. Try and get the manicure clients on the nail envy
6. Make your hand massage a relaxing time. Take your time and introduce the spa manicure.
7. Have the clients feeling better when they leave than they did coming into your salon.

Foot treatments

- Spray feet with sanitizer and alcohol (use gloves if you want)
- Use mango exfoliant apply to feet
- Place bag on feet sit for 5 to 10 minutes
- Remove bag use warm towels to remove exfoliant
- Next use moisturizer and massage feet
- A little filing to clean ends of nails
- Apply mango oil to cuticles and rub in to nails for shiny a finish

Spa Treatments Tips

Not Busy?! Take some moisturizer and give someone else's client a hand massage! Apply next of skin to tone, smooth, and buff dry skin.

Cuticle oil: Go over to the client and ask if you can apply oil to the cuticle. Talk about our hot oil treatment.

Spa Soak: Put a few drops of aromatherapy oil in a dish and ask clients to soak for a minute or two. This is great while perm is sitting or color, while waiting at the reception area, or while under the dryer.

This makes time go faster when not busy, makes our salon known for treating our clients, makes more money, and you may get more clients. Clients like to be pampered!

It's All About the Spa Day!

Tips and Tricks

Face: Feel beautiful on the go; give yourself a natural soft glow with baked bronzer. Create a sun kissed look from day to night.

Hair: Shiny silky hair, create a vibrant more radiant gloss to your hair. Color me glosser or shine serum to protect and enhance sheen.

Nails: Are your hands dry, flaky, rough? Why not give them a dip into a more youthful look. Paraffin dips are a great way to soften, firm, and protect your hand from the harsh environment. So come on, take a dip.

Skin Care: Seven genetic skin types
1. **Very Dry Skin:** thin texture, closed pores, transparent, dehydrated
2. **Dry Skin:** low oil, small pores, thin texture
3. **Combination Dry Skin:** medium to thick texture, normal pores, t-zone oiliness in nose area
4. **Combination Normal Skin:** mildly oily, medium texture, normal to large pores, t-zone oiliness
5. **Combination Oily:** moderately oily, medium to thick texture, comedones (blackheads)
6. **Oily Skin:** extremely oily, thick texture, large pores
7. **Seborrheic Skin:** greasy, thick, large pores

Health and Wellness

Your Lifestyle

Eight hours of sleep per night is recommended. How many do you usually get? _____

Regular exercise is essential for good health. Do you have a routine? _____

Nutrition

Drink enough water daily and monitor caffeine intake. Do you drink enough water? _____

Do you eat enough fresh fruits and vegetables each day? _____

Health

Would you say you have high stress levels on a daily basis? _____

Do you take a vitamin supplements? Ask your doctor what is best. _____

Personal Care

Do you use body moisturizers on a regular basis? _____

Do you cleanse, moisturize, and use sunblock on your face daily? _____

Did you know?:
- Deep breathing calms the nervous system and relaxes the body.
- White spots on your nails are related to injuries to the base (matrix) of the nail. The spots will disappear as your nails grow.
- The lack of vitamin B can cause hair loss. Eat more beans, nuts, and eggs.
- To keep your face clean and clear, you should cleanse, tone, and moisturize daily.
- Eczema may be caused by allergies to medications, food, or chemicals.
- Alopecia can be caused by traumatic shock to the nervous system or nutritional deficiencies.
- Nail biting is a nervous habit and one of the most common causes of deformed nails.
- Blue nails are a sign of poor blood circulation.
- To keep your hair in great condition, you should get a haircut every 5 to 7 weeks.
- A deep stimulating scalp treatment will increase blood flow to the scalp and will help promote growth and maximize moisture in the hair.
- Oily or dry dandruff should be treated with medicated shampoo until the condition improves.
- You should exfoliate your skin on your face once per week to prevent pore blockage.
- Surrounding yourself with vibrant color will uplift your mood.

Chapter 13

Jacqueline's Inside Out

Education

What is the Inside Out Education Program? Our program is designed to educate, motivate, and inspire stylists to pursue their dreams. The main goal of the program is to bring stylists together as a team so that we can network and share ideas and insights on salon issues.

Jacqueline's inside out program is a team effort. When you put together events, training workshops, and mentoring programs this does require lots of preparation, team work and dedicated individuals who work hard to get the job done. Over the past few years of starting Jacqueline's Inside Out Through the program I have developed relationships and built a team of stylists, along with teachers and educators to develop a group of Pittsburgh's finest in the beauty industry. We have now added a photographer and fashion designer to our team. Again, developing relationships no matter what industry you are seeking is a very important task to grow and reach new levels of business. Networking within your field and reaching out to other businesses will keep you in touch with new clients and help you to continue to make connections to grow your business. Remember that you cannot operate a successful business without the combined efforts of a good team. The group of people in my program has been a tremendous help to me. They have contributed to my growth, and I thank them for their dedication and effort they put forth in the future of the beauty industry.

Vision
Mentoring with a Twist

JACQUELINE'S INSIDE OUT
EDUCATION PROGRAM

Vision

- Professional hair designers networking, together as a team, dedicated to expanding their knowledge
- Leading the way through education, inspiration, and mentoring
- Growing relationships and building a successful salon for the future

Mission

- Combining our individual strengths and talents to share the goals and passion for our industry
- Having a strong reputation for leading the way by example of our quality, respect, and success for education and growth

Goals

- Striving for success in this industry
- Growing, educating, and developing into a team of Pittsburgh's finest hair designers
- Thinking ahead to the future and never losing sight of our vision or mission
- Having our association known for its education, talent, and knowledge
- Help our salon and our sales grow as well

JACQUELINE'S INSIDE OUT
EDUCATION PROGRAM

1. Foundation
2. Mission
3. Vision
4. Values
5. Training and Membership Program
6. Strategy
7. Team Building and Coaching
8. Recruitment
9. Process Overview
10. Policy and Procedure Handbook

These ten steps are the focus of Jacqueline's Inside Out Education Program.

Business Builders

Back to Basics
- Education
- Inspiration
- Motivation

Launch Our First Show or Class
- Focus on the power of salon, service, and basics of the business.
- In-salon classes
- Schools or shows
- Advanced education

Growth for the Future
- Inspire - Learn - Commitment - Skill

JACQUELINE'S INSIDE OUT

EDUCATION PROGRAM

1. **Foundation:**
   - What is our identity?
   - How were we built?
   - _____
   - _____

2. **Mission:**
   - What are we trying to achieve?
   - Why are we here?
   - _____
   - _____

3. **Vision:**
   - What are we trying to develop?
   - Understanding our position
   - _____
   - _____

4. **Values:**
   - What really matters?
   - How to achieve excellence
   - _____
   - _____

5. **Training and Mentoring Program:**
   - How to be inspiring
   - Create a wonderful industry
   - _____
   - _____

6. **Strategy:**
   - Our plan
   - How are we going to get there?
   - _____
   - _____

7. **Team Building and Coaching:**
   - Leadership qualities
   - Meeting, evaluations, feedback
   - _____
   - _____

8. **Recruitment:**
   - Apprenticeship
   - Beauty School
   - _____
   - _____

9. **Process Overview:**
   - Building our Team and our Board
   - Education – Becoming a Team
   - _____
   - _____

10. **Policy and Procedure Handbook:**
    - Regulations
    - _____
    - _____
    - _____

Chapter 14

Inside Out Mentor Program
What is Inside Out?

MENTORING WITH A TWIST!

Hello! My name is **Shaylee Capatolla**, and I am the daughter of **Jacqueline's Salon** owner, **Jacqueline Capatolla**. Since my mother is a salon owner of over 16 years, one could say that I grew up in the hair salon. And, although I have a true passion for the field of cosmetology, I chose to follow in her footsteps in a "round about" way. Rather than attending cosmetology school, I opted for a degree in Psychology from the University of Pittsburgh. After graduating in 2009 I have been heavily involved with the planning and execution of a wonderful new program. As co-owners of **Jacqueline's Inside-Out** program, my mother and I are combining our skills to bring women "Mentoring with a Twist!" Our unique program will include inspirational speakers, friendship building, makeup, hair & fashion tutorials, and much, much more! Inside-Out has been specially designed to teach the importance of inner beauty first! So many females experience the same feelings and emotions throughout their lifetimes. It is time to work together as women and overcome our innermost insecurities. With my mother's talents in the beauty industry, and my knowledge of the human mind, we feel that together we can and will make a difference in the lives of women everywhere. Our hope is that you will join us on this remarkable journey! Visit our website at http://www.jacquelinesnews.com/insideout.html.

-Shaylee Capatolla

Hello! My name is Shaylee Capatolla and I am the daughter of Jacqueline's Salon owner, Jacqueline Capatolla. Being that my mother is a salon owner of over 18 years, one could say that I grew up in the hair salon. And, although I have a solid passion for the field of cosmetology, I chose to follow in her footsteps in a "round about" way. Rather than attending cosmetology school, I opted for a degree in Psychology from the University of Pittsburgh in 2009. Upon my graduation I have been heavily involved with the planning and execution of a wonderful new program. As co-owners of Jacqueline's Inside-Out, my mother and I are combing our skills to bring women of all ages "Mentoring with a Twist!" Our unique program includes inspirational speakers, friendship building, makeup, hair & fashion tutorials, and much, much more! Inside-Out has been specially designed to teach the importance of inner beauty first! Many of us experience similar emotions throughout a lifetime. It is time to work together and overcome those inner most insecurities. With my mother's talents in the beauty industry, and my knowledge of the human mind, we feel as though together we can and will make a difference! Sign up below to be notified of any upcoming events!

☐ motivational speakers ☐ goal set advising ☐ friendship building
☐ female empowerment ☐ beauty consultations ☐ hair styling tips ☐ makeup tutorials
☐ fashion's latest trends

What is Inside Out?

The Inside Out Program was created by Jacqueline and Shaylee to help women empower themselves. A portion of the proceeds from our efforts will be donated to a cause for women within our community.

Beauty shines through every human being in many ways. A smile, a helping hand, a good deed—all of these are ways that can encourage and strengthen those around us.

Stay tuned for the next Word of the Month and begin to take part in an exciting adventure as Inside Out and give inspiration, hope, and a desire to restore healthy values in the lives of women.

Thank you,

Jacqueline Capatolla

INSIDE OUT MENTORING PROGRAM

Learn to Love Yourself

- **Mission**
  - For all of us to feel the love for ourselves for the beautiful women they are inside and out!
- **Vision**
  - To spread beauty and love inside and out one woman at a time
- **Goals**
  - To be able to give back to the community and help women to lift themselves up to a better place in life
  - To see the glow in the eyes of every woman when she sees herself in a new light
- **Targeting**
  - Any woman who wishes to have confidence and a healthy self-esteem
  - All women who wish to come out of any dark and unpleasant period of their lives and head in a more positive direction
  - Every woman who desires to be happy and fulfilled

D = DESIRE
R = RESPECT
E = EDUCATION
A = ATTITUDE
M = MENTOR

Chapter 15

Event Planning

Jacqueline's Team Plan of Action

- To Attend Workshops
- Join Training
- List of potential clients (names, emails, addresses, phone numbers)
- Be prepared to promote yourself
- Summer campaign
- Fall results
- Set goals
- STAY MOTIVATED AND FOCUSED!

Vendor Application

- Please Arrive at 11:30 a.m. for Vendor check in and set up
- A table will be reserved with your business name on it for you to decorate as you wish
- Guests will begin to arrive at 12:30 p.m.
- The event will run from 1:00-5:00 p.m.
- Checks can be made payable to: Jacqueline's Salon
- Please mail to: Jacqueline's Salon, 310 Grant Street, Suite 107, Pittsburgh, PA 15219
- Please feel free to call Jacqueline or Shaylee at (412) 281-2209 with any questions

THURSDAY, NOVEMBER 17, 2011

TIME: 6PM-8PM

JACQUELINE'S GLITZ AND GLAM

KICK OFF THE HOLIDAYS!
$10 INCLUDES

HOW TO LESSON
LOOK-N-LEARN
REFRESHMENTS
PRIZES

$30 OR MORE IN PRODUCTS=A FREE BROW WAX !
BOGO %25 OFF DEALS
HOLIDAY STOCKING STUFFERS
GRAB BAG GIFT IDEAS
$50 GIFT CARD=$5 FREE

BROOKLINE LOCATION!!!

WWW.JACQUELINESNEWS.COM

Holiday Kick-off

Glitz and Glam

HOLIDAY GLOW

BRIGHTEN YOUR SPIRITS AND YOUR FACE WITH
THE HOLIDAY GLOW RETEXTURIZING TREATMENT.
THIS 100% NATURAL, GENTLE PROCEDURE EXFOLIATES
DEAD SKIN CELLS WHILE RENEWING THE TEXTURE AND
CLARITY OF YOUR SKIN. YOUR HOLIDAY BEAUTY REGIME
SHOULD BEGIN BY DRAMATICALLY IMPROVING THE
FOUNDATION OF YOUR SKIN WITH THE HOLDAY GLOW
RETEXTURIZING TREATMENT. SPECIAL FEATURE HOT ROCKS.

1 HOUR $65.00

Chapter 16

We've Got Cows!

What in the world does this mean and how does it relate to a hair salon? (I know you are thinking that). Well, we all get those crazy times in the salon. Ok, you want to be professional, but sometimes things just go badly. My nail technician had a lot of friends (which included a former husband), and on occasion, the whole group of them would visit the salon. One day, as I was cutting my client's hair, the barber was shaving his client's face, and the nail technician was giving a manicure, the door suddenly burst open and the nail technician's former husband and the brigade of friends entered the salon carrying a microwave, a huge basket, fur coats, and a baby stroller. One of the friends asked to use the restroom. All three of us had been focused on the work we were doing with our clients, but I must admit that our concentration was broken a bit by this bizarre parade of people and activity. Did you ever see the movie, "Twister," when the people are driving in a car near the funnel cloud? The cows were blowing all around them in the air and a woman says, *We've got cows…,* indicating that all control was lost and everything went nuts! That day, I took my salon manager aside and I said, *Oh my, I feel like I'm in the movie, Twister!* I wondered how all of this could be happening at once." All of us quickly regained our composure and continued our work, but it that moment, that I realized how important it is to pull in the reins when and if unusual activity occurs during the workday. When this incident occurred, I remained calm and reassuring to my new client during her first visit to my salon. I did not want her to think that my salon always has a circus-like atmosphere.

It has become an inside joke with my salon manager on those days when things get a little chaotic. We find ourselves saying, *We've Got Cows!* We will always remember that day of mayhem, and it remains one of my favorite salon stories!

We've Got Cows!

When bizarre things happen during our workday, my salon manager and I always say, We've Got Cows, like in the movie, Twister. It has become an inside joke!

OMG! Is she dead in the tanning bed? "Hello" "Wake Up"

Oh no, is she actually going to follow me into the ladies' room and keep asking me questions about her hair?

What is that noise?

Is Betty snoring under the dryer?

Did that lady really have tape holding her face back?

What was that?!!!

Keep Smiling!

Fun Times

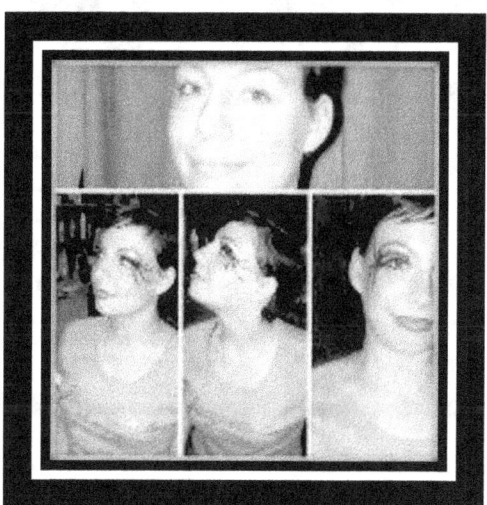

Work should be fun!

Fun Times

With Prom Girls Gone Wild

I love prom days--teens on the phone texting the whole time I'm doing their hair, teens fighting with their mom on how to wear their hair and about what they are doing after the prom. The moms usually look like they have been through the wringer and are totally exhausted. I have done an entire up-do on a young woman only to hear her say, *I changed my mind, I want to wear it like Ashley's hair, can you please do it over? Sure,* you say, as your next prom girl is staring you down because she needs to have her photos taken in a half hour. Seriously, prom time is a great opportunity to show your creative side and to bring in more revenue for the salon. It is a lot of fun doing up-styles and makeup. It is a time for you as a designer to step out of the box and try something more rewarding. The whole package for prom and weddings is a special way for you to show your artistic ability and challenge yourself to new heights. We always offer a prom package, and we give our clients a great experience for their special day.

Classic / Couture

Shout Outs to Clients

Ten Shout Outs!

1. **Nancy.** Thanks for all the great vacation stories. Love to hear about those adventures.
2. **Louie.** You are the best to make the salon hop with all of your jokes!
3. **Sue.** I never know what you will say! And I love it how you make me smile!
4. **Marian.** You are the most fashionable client. I love to see what you will have on next time!
5. **Rose.** My creative client. I love that I get to do whatever style I want!
6. **Barb.** You are so down to earth and so interesting to talk to… thanks.
7. **Steve.** Wow! What great marketing advice. Thank you!
8. **Sandy.** I love to hear all about your children and grandchildren. We have grown together!
9. **Eileen.** You always crack me up with you dry sense of humor! I love it.
10. **David.** Thanks for always asking about my family and my day!
11. **Pearl.** It is always a pleasure to talk to you. You have a way of making others feel calm!
12. Special shout out to all of my clients! Thank you for your loyalty! Jacqueline

Shout Outs to Girlfriends

We all need a friend. Friends are essential to have in your life when you need someone to talk to and to laugh with. We also need our friends when life brings misfortunes our way. I love getting together with my friends. We catch up with each other about our families and how things are going in our careers. We reserve time to get together even though our busy lives leave little extra time. Setting aside some time for friends is worth every effort. My dear friends, I hope that we have many years together. I treasure all of you because you have all been there for me, and I am grateful that you are just a phone call away.

Thank you to all my girlfriends!

Love, Jackie

Conclusion

Jacqueline's 2

It is hard for me to believe that I own two salons. When I opened my first salon, I put all my energy in to it to make it a success, never thinking I would do it all again. When the opportunity arose for me to open my second salon, I knew it would be a lot of hard work. I was up for the challenge. I feel like you won't get anywhere in life if you don't take chances, or if you let opportunities pass you by. You need to find your place in this industry. Being a salon owner is not for everyone and that's ok. Salon ownership is challenging and rewarding. Opening and owning a salon requires the right blend of energy, time, talent, money, and courage. You need to be prepared for what will be expected of you once you open your doors to your first client. Keep in mind, that there is a lot of competition in this business, and that the right balance of creativity and business sense determines the success of your salon.

You will need to consult experts about all aspects of your business. Take some time to learn about the good suppliers, and seek a respected distributer who employs a good sales representative who can help you with product support, training, and education. Sales associates are a great asset to your business. They will help you to increase your profit margin. They will also work with you on promotional ideas, event planning, and product support. Make sure you deal with a manufacturer who has your best interest in mind, and one that will offer the most knowledge and client support.

Going through this journey with you has been a pleasure. I enjoyed sharing my experiences with you and it is my hope is that you will get at least one thing out of this book to help you with the process of following your dreams. Refer to this manual and keep it close to you. When times get tough or you need some encouragement, take another look. Read some of the chapters more than once. Sometimes a second look will cause a light bulb to go off, and you will get a tip that you either missed or one that you just needed to read again. As I said in the beginning of this, I wish for you to figure out who you are as a person, an individual, and a stylist. Whatever road you take in your career path, remember that if you put your heart and soul into it and it succeeds then you will know that you made the right decision. Keep in mind that there are times when we make plans in life that just don't work out, or they run their course. When a plan or dream comes to an end, you should be grateful for the learning experience, and not view this as a failure. If, in time, you come to a point that you need to enter into a new chapter in your life, be excited for the new adventure and also give yourself credit for being brave enough to take another a new direction. They say, in life, when God closes one door another one will open. We need to trust in that and have faith that all good things happen for the right reason.

I wish for you to know that you can take on your goals and dreams and go forward with them. Start the process today. Don't put it off, get out there and live and love your life. This positive thinking has helped me during the times when I needed to pick myself up and move forward. Writing my thoughts and ideas down has been a great way for me to express who I am. I thank you for listening and being a part of my dream and my goals.

May God Bless You Always!
Jacqueline Capatolla ☺

Follow Your Dreams!

Commitment and Passion

Business

Dormont, Brookline Business Owners Win Awards

Cassandra Gillen and Jacqueline Capatolla were recipients of WSBA awards in April.

By Erin Faulk Email the author April 17, 2012

Tweet   Email   Print   1 Comment

Related Topics: Cassandra Gillen, Cassandra's Florals, Jacqueline Capatolla, Jacqueline's House of Beauty, and WSBA Award

The Women's Small Business Association has named two local women among its top women business owners of 2012.

Cassandra Gillen, owner of Cassandra's Florals on West Liberty Avenue in Dormont, was named the 2012 WSBA Woman of the Year. Jacqueline Capatolla, owner of Jacqueline's House of Beauty on Brookline Boulevard in Brookline, was named the 2012 WSBA Best Business Woman in Pittsburgh.

Although the awards were different, the criteria was similar – both required business owners to show professionalism and quality in their own business, as well as support to their communities and to other local businesses.

Owning a small business is hard work, the women said, but the "giving" part of the job seems to come easily to both.

Capatolla has participated in events with the Brookline Chamber of Commerce and the South Pittsburgh Development Corporation. Her staff also has collected canned goods and sponsored basket raffles for the Brookline food pantry, and has donated products to Mom's House of Pittsburgh. She is in the process of writing a book about starting a new business.

She also started Jacqueline's Inside Out program, with the goal of helping young women establish confidence and self esteem. Together with her daughter, Capatolla has hosted or helped organize events that feature makeovers, motivational speakers, mentoring female students, and helping women prepare for job interviews.

"We want to help women feel better inside about themselves," Capatolla said. "Here, we can help with outside beauty, which we've done, but we want to help them have that inner confidence, too."

Gillen also has quite the resume of service work.

Her eclectic floral shop is, as she says, "not your grandmother's florist." In addition to her work as a full-service florist, Gillen also sells antiques, jewelry, bath products, hand-poured candles, greeting cards and other items in her store. Many items are handmade locally, and each display is accompanied by the business cards of other women business owners.

"This store is me," she said. "It's a representation of everything I love. When you have something in the community, you have to welcome people in. You have to be welcoming and invite people to be part of it."

Gillen started a "Change for Change" program. She has made either monetary donations or donated floral arrangements to Friends of Dormont Pool, the Dormont Athletic Boosters Association, Dig Dormont, Dormont Public Library, Mt. Lebanon High School marching band, the American Heart Association's Heart Ball, Pittsburgh Social Exchange, Dress for Success and the Cystic Fibrosis Foundation.

"It all goes back to treating others as you want to be treated," Gillen said. "If I can help somebody, I will."

Gillen said her business is always growing and changing, and Capatolla's is, too - she recently opened a second location for her business in Downtown Pittsburgh. Both women said they were surprised and honored to receive their awards.

"I was surrounded by women in the same position as me," Capatolla said. "I just told them I was happy to be there, and that it was an honor to get the award, with everyone there trying to accomplish the same things."

Follow Dormont-Brookline Patch on Facebook and Twitter. For more information, sign up for our email Newsletter.

ONE OF THE ARTICLES THAT I HAVE WRITTEN FOR A LOCAL NEWSPAPER

BEAUTY AND FASHION GLAM

Welcome to SPRING...as we get ready to smell the fresh flowers, and hear the sounds of the birds in the morning, and feel that breeze as we take that walk in the park. Remember to take it all in, to enjoy the fresh new season. April may be the month of showers, but it can also mean a cleansing of your mind and body. Think of this as a time to get rid of all those toxins that have been weighing you down.

To cleanse your mind of heartbreak, insecurities, and hatred...use this time to re-focus your energy on simplifying your life and enjoying the things that make you happy! Take time to smell the roses, and really listen to those birds, and the children playing at the park. These are the moments that matter and make you feel like you are really living life.

Speaking of cleansing... Did you know that your face needs a good cleansing daily? You should remember to cleanse, tone and moisturize your skin every day to keep your skin vibrant and fresh. Why not try that facial to help get your skin in tip top shape? Yes it is time to pretty up those toes. It's pedicure time; flip flops are calling your name. SPRING is a time to brighten up that color...OMBRE color is what's hot now. This is a tone on tone color that goes from one tone to the other softly as it blends out. The color of the season...coral and mustard colors will be very popular along with the floral prints, so brighten up those outfits!!

Get your new spring style... Brighten up and CLEANSE your mind and body! Simplify, and take time to enjoy life!

Until next time ...live your dreams!

Jacqueline Capatolla, **Jacqueline's Salon**

www.jacquelinesnews.com

Reach for the Stars

Hard work and dedication will bring many rewards!

Credits

Jordan Gustine
Bethany Hensel
Hair and Beauty Industry
Pittsburgh Beauty Academy
Debi Weiss, Owner of Fashion and Designer Gallery Intl
State Board of Cosmetology
Google™ — Facebook – Twitter

Inspiration from the following fashion magazines: Allure, FrontRow Monthly Modern Salon, Launch Pad, Behind the Chair, American Salon

Manufacturers: Matrix, OPI, Paul Mitchell, Crew, Nexus, Wella, Redkin, Tressa, Creative, Sexy Hair, Soyil Candles

Movie Credits: *Twister* (1996) - for the script reference to *We've Got Cows*

Production Companies: Warner Bros. Pictures (presents) (as Warner Bros.) / Universal Pictures (presents) / Amblin Entertainment (as an Amblin Entertainment production) / Constant c Productions

Photo Credits to: HK Photo Studio, Edwin Shaw Photography, Melissa Distal Photography – Pittsburgh Fashion Week, Barry Felix – Jet Productions Photography, Angie Candell, Gina Caruso Hussar

Radio Station: K-Love, 2012 Media Education Foundation

Jacqueline's Salon Team of Stylists and Makeup Artists

Molly Beurkle
Cindy Cazin
Eric Hargrove
Jordan McGee
Billy Joseph
Sandra Joseph
Katrina Mustakas
Brazil Raine
Kim Rohanna
Students from the A.W. Beattie Career Center

Models:

Shaylee Capatolla
Nicole Clites
Katie D'Arcangelo
Savannah Kennick
Elena LaQuatra
Isabella LaQuatra
Allyn Lewis
Jillian Markovic
Celina Pompeani
Annie Rosellini
Abby Stefanski
Heather Weston

Manuscript Preparation

Maggie Cauley

Publications / Organizatons:

The Brookline Chamber of Commerce
The BROOKline Newsletter
Linda Boss of A. Boss
Dormont / Brookline Patch Newsletter
WSBA – Women's Small Business Association
City of Pittsburgh Proclamation Award

616 Brookline Blvd.
Pittsburgh, Pa 15226
Phone: (412) 281-2209
E-mail: shaylee@jacquelinesnews.com
www.jacquelinesnews.com

Grant Building Lobby---Suite 107
310-300 Grant Street
Pittsburgh, PA 15219

Phone: (412) 281-2209
E-mail: shaylee@jacquelinesnews.com
www.jacquelinesnews.com

**Thank you for visiting
Jacqueline's Salons!**

Until next time, live your dreams.

Jacqueline Capatolla

www.ingramcontent.com/pod-product-compliance
Lightning Source LLC
Chambersburg PA
CBHW081141170526
45165CB00008B/2757